ManageHub

The step-by-step business breakthrough strategy.

Michael S. Kramer, CPA

ManageHub Press

ManageHub™
The step-by-step business breakthrough strategy.
Published by ManageHub Press a division of tsWB Strategies, Inc. Skokie, IL
www.managehub.com
Copyright © 2013 by tsWB Strategies, Inc., Skokie, IL

For general information on our other products and services, please contact our Business Development Department in the U.S. at 800-999-9231.

ISBN- 978-0-9899086-2-7

Manufactured in the United States of America

Please visit us online for more free tools:

ManageHub.info
&
BreakthroughProject.com

Table of Contents

Dear Reader,

Quality management practices are widely viewed as the key to innovation, consistent quality, employee engagement, customer satisfaction, increased profitability, rapid growth and maximizing success. They offer entrepreneurs and business leaders a mountain of wisdom to optimize and transform their companies. Yet, too few businesses climb the mountain. They are either unfamiliar with quality-management models or are unable to turn theory into practice. This is a detriment to their companies, whose success is unpredictable. It is also a detriment to their communities, who rely on small businesses to fuel employment and GDP. Given the recent economic data, this is truer than ever.

The mission of the Breakthrough Project is to help business owners use quality-management practices to dramatically improve their chances of success. To do this we want to create a worldwide movement where business owners and managers can find the tools they need to build solid, sustainable and scalable companies that benefit their communities, their employees and themselves.

To date, over 10,000 copies of the original Breakthrough Book have been downloaded. We are proud to release this special ManageHub edition. Please create your free ManageHub.com account and use it to create your company's management framework.

How You Can Help:

The heart and soul of our movement is our Breakthrough Community. Our community includes college-based Entrepreneurship Centers, State and National Quality Award Programs, Small Business Development Centers, business coaches, quality consultants, accountants, and business journalists, bloggers and activists. Our community shares a passion for helping businesses succeed. They are blogging, reporting, and tweeting links to this book, the eight free Breakthrough management tools, free cloud-based ManageHub.com management software, and our growing list of business success stories. We ask you to join us by helping spread the word and/or by sponsoring a ManageHub Chapter in your community.

If we work together, we can change the world… one business at a time.

Looking Forward,

Michael Kramer, CPA

Join the movement: www.breakthroughproject.com

Create your ManageHub account: www.managehub.com

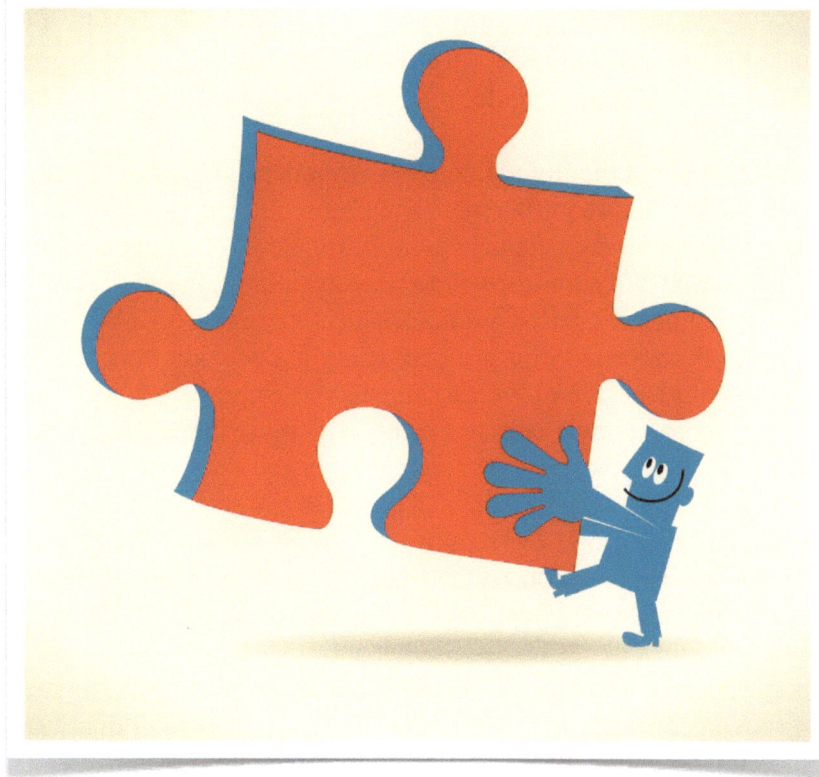

Chapter One:
Commit to Building Your Company's Management Framework

What are Best Management Practices?

For the last sixty years, the greatest business minds have been exploring, theorizing and fine-tuning a body of knowledge collectively known as "quality management practices." You may be familiar with quality-management through the work of thought leaders like W. Edwards Deming[i] and Joseph Juran[ii]. You may have read classic management books like "The Goal[iii]," "Good to Great[iv]" and "E-Myth[v]." You may have even attempted quality-management approaches like U.S. Baldrige Performance Excellence Program[vi],

EFQM[vii] (The European Foundation for Quality Management), TQM[viii] (Total Quality Management), Kaizen[ix], Six-Sigma[x], ISO[xi] (International Standards Organization), or CMMI[xii] (Capabilities Maturity Model Integration).

The more you learn about quality management practices, the more you realize that they share common themes and requirements. Their most fundamental shared requirement is that you create your company's management framework. A management framework automates your company's *management processes* in the same way accounting software automates bookkeeping, or a CRM automates customer relations. With consistent use, your management framework helps your company become very organized, efficient, and continually improving. Your employees can become empowered, self-motivated, and self-managed. Your company's culture can become more innovative, focused, and collaborative.

In his best-selling book, "Good-to-Great," Jim Collins refers to the concept of a management framework as a "consistent system." The U.S. Baldrige Performance Excellence Program, and EFQM call it a "leadership framework." Other quality management approaches like ISO, Six Sigma, and CMMI fill in the gaps. They emphasize key concepts like process standardization, employee engagement, and continual improvement. They may emphasize different aspects of quality-management, but they all require an overarching, automated management framework.

Why Do You Need a Management Framework?

To understand the importance of creating your company's management framework, consider what makes a great company, GREAT!

From a customer's point of view, a great business is efficient. Its quality is consistent. Customers are treated like royalty. It is clean. It is organized. It is creative, innovative and imaginative. Its employees are happy, and it is very profitable.

From a leader's point of view, a great business implements a set of internal systems that it uses to manage all its moving parts. Successfully managing these systems allows the business to maximize its success:

- **Processes:** Systematized, standardized, and continually improved.
- **Leadership:** Ensure people, processes, and strategies are aligned and operating consistently and with excellence.
- **Knowledge Management:** Information gets to the right people at the right time.
- **Strategy:** Business objectives are organically created, communicated and updated.
- **Communication/Collaboration:** Stakeholders have an equal voice and an equal opportunity to make a difference.
- **Employees:** Hire, onboard, and groom your best people for advancement.

- **Culture:** Promotes quality, innovation, and open communication, and active engagement.
- **Values:** Communicates a set of behaviors that all employees are required to consistently demonstrate.
- **Project Management:** One, company-wide system to implement internal, strategic improvement initiatives.
- **Results:** Key performance indicators measure and report results in real-time.

Most organizations invest significant time and money building management systems related to some, if not all of the above, elements. For example, they may employ an elaborate strategic planning process. They may have a project management system. They may use a knowledgebase or wiki. They may have a host of stand-alone communication systems ranging from emails to blogs. Their latest addition may be a collaboration system.

Even when using all of the above tools, leaders wonder why they still suffer from the same set of frustrating management problems:

- Dissatisfied customers
- Inconsistent quality
- Disgruntled employees
- Lost knowledge
- Miscommunication
- Misaligned strategies
- Derailed projects
- Politicking
- Employee resistance to improvement
- Inefficient operations
- Inability to break through
- Disorganization
- Recurring problems
- Lack of transparency
- Lack of accountability
- Lack of innovation
- Inability to scale
- Stress

The problem is that most of the management tools (project management tools, knowledge systems, strategic planning systems, etc.) exist in silos. They may be state-of-the-art, but they do not work together to create an automated "management framework."

To illustrate the relationship between the required management elements, draw a line between each related item:

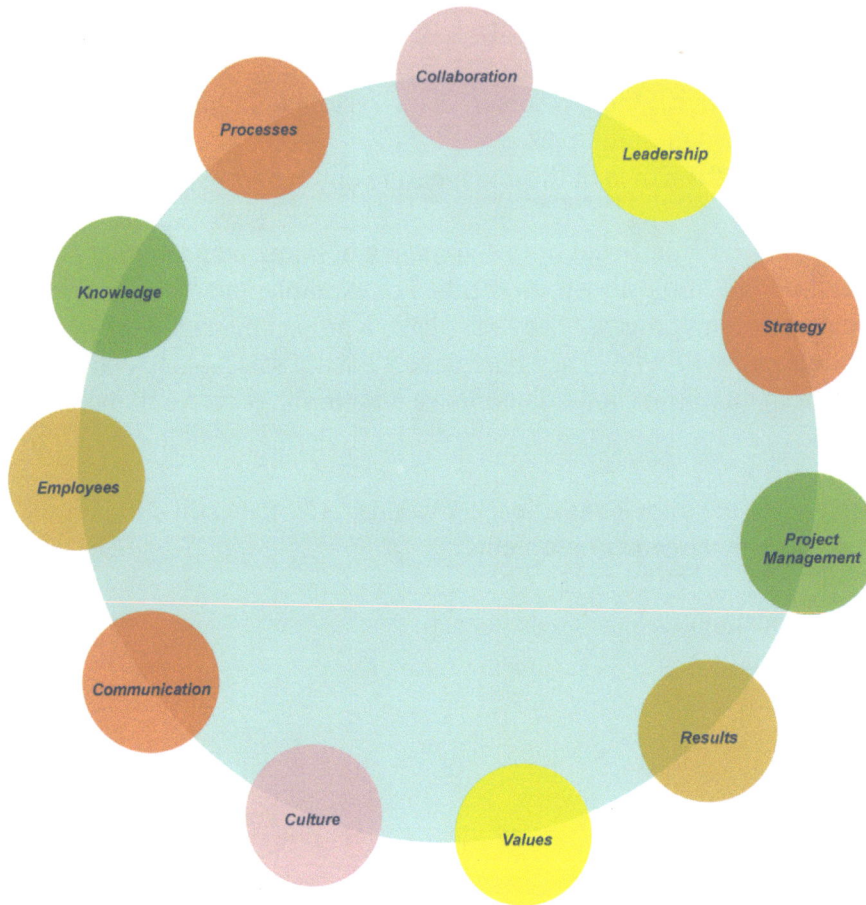

For example, you would need to draw a line from the *Process Management* circle to all of the following related circles:

- **Knowledge:** Processes need well documented policies, procedures, training methods and forms.
- **Employees:** Process teams must actively document and improve their processes.
- **Communication:** Employees need ways to share their ideas for improving processes.
- **Culture:** Employees must be willing to document and improve their processes.
- **Values:** The Company needs to promote the discipline of process standardization and improvement.
- **Results:** Process teams need ways to measure performance and improvement.
- **Project Management:** Employees need ways to manage projects dedicated to process improvement.
- **Strategy:** Each process needs a clearly defined improvement objective.
- **Leadership:** Senior leaders must support and monitor process excellence.
- **Collaboration:** Process-teams need ways to collaborate with internal and external resources to improve their processes.

As you continue connecting circles, you notice that every management element is connected to each other. Once complete, your illustration looks like the following:

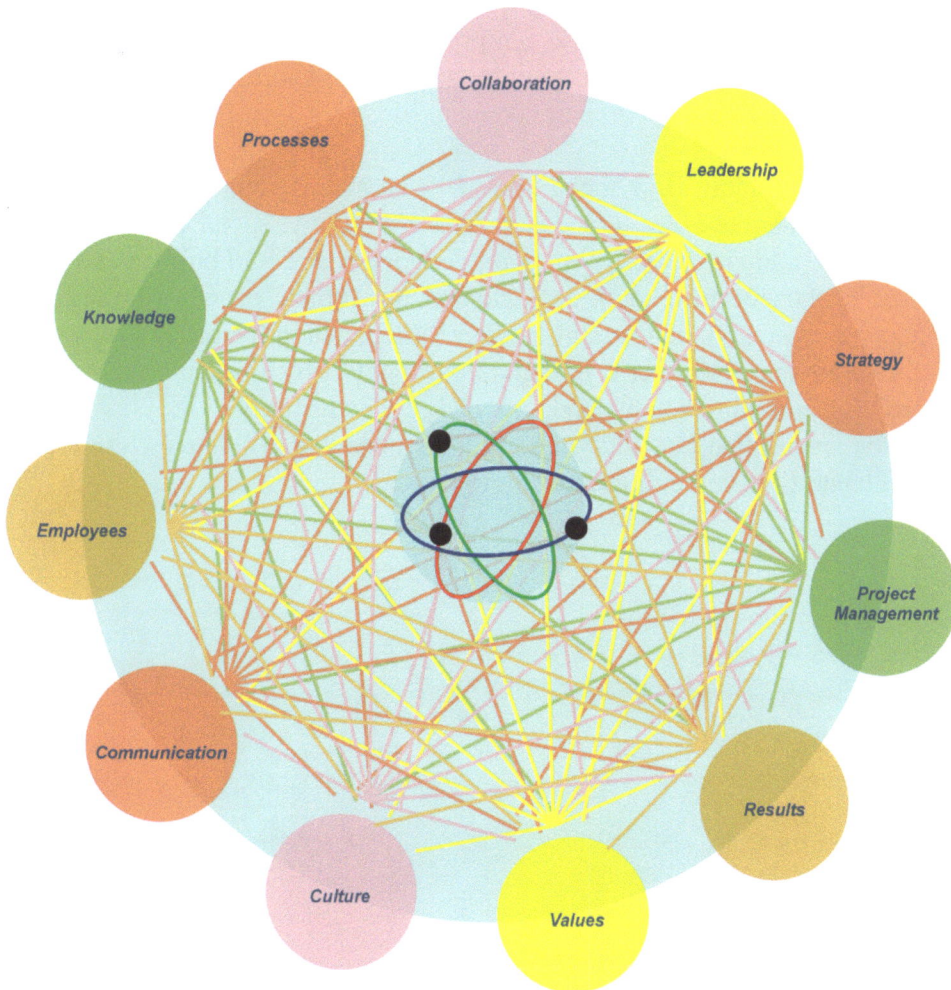

This exercise illustrates why most organizations struggle to implement quality management practices. It seems impossible to create an integrated system that can effectively manage all of the necessary relationships.

The difficulty of applying basic management theory is acknowledged by most quality-management approaches. For example, the U.S. Baldrige Performance Excellence Program and EFQM describe their models as "non-prescriptive." This means that although they provide a comprehensive theoretical "framework," it is up to you to create the internal management systems needed to bring their frameworks to life.

Other popular quality-management methods like Six Sigma, ISO, and CMMI, require extensive and expensive training. They are so complex that they are out of reach of most organizations.

ManageHub changes this.

ManageHub is a Ready-to-Use Management Framework

ManageHub is an internet-based social-enterprise application that makes it easy to create your company's management framework. Simply create your account and load your company's unique characteristics: departments, processes, people, strategies, projects, and knowhow. Then, watch your company come to life.

ManageHub features an innovative social interface that makes your management framework "sticky." The interface includes everyone's favorite social elements like newsfeeds, face-grids, blogs, search, collaborative workspaces, and built-in auto-responders that send users email reminders and updates. It then leverages these features to interconnect the required management elements, (depicted in the circle graphics above), to give users one click access to their departments, processes, employees, strategies, projects, communications, and knowledge. The result is a ready-made management framework that you and your employees can use to create a culture of innovation, collaboration, and continuous improvement.

With one click:
- Create a project,
- Assign a task,
- Share knowledge,
- Start a discussion
- Create a group,
- Send an in-mail.

Facegrid connects you to everyone.

Link boxes connect you to all of your collaboration workspaces:
- Departments
- Processes
- Groups
- Projects
- ComLogs
- Groups

Your activity-feed provides you with links to everything that has changed that relates to your work.

Click on any activity-feed link to access the related workspace.

Use ManageHub to become very organized. Use it to plan and implement your business strategies. Use it to document your company's know-how. Use it to free your employees from their "job traps" so they can grow with your business. Use it to expand your business, open new markets, and create new products. Use it to eliminate waste, reduce errors, and create an efficient, lean-operating business. Use it to reduce the need for meetings, conference calls, and email. Use it to improve product quality, consistency and customer satisfaction. Use it to free yourself from working 24-7-365 so you can focus on business building… and enjoy your life.

Above all, use your new ManageHub leadership framework to create a *common management language* for your company. Instead of the chaos of every manager and every team having their own way of managing, you and your employees will have one, universal company-way of managing. This simplified and standardized management approach allows participants to easily move from team to team and support any manager in any department, process, project or group/committee.

Adopting a *common management language* yields significant benefits including increased organizational flexibility, resilience, and collaboration. It reduces politicking, improves team performance, and increases employee satisfaction. It also helps create *generations of leaders* where all participants learn how to manage people, processes, and strategies at the department, process, and employee levels. Their leadership skills can develop organically as they move from managing project tasks, to managing project-teams, to managing process-areas, and ultimately, to managing departments. As your leadership framework matures, you can adopt a policy of hiring employees at the bottom and promoting them to the top. This will further engage and reward employees. It also creates a nimble and low cost workforce that is highly scalable.

The remainder of this book provides you and your employees with an easy onramp to adopting quality-management practices and creating your company's *common management language*. It is a practical approach that includes step-by-step instructions about how to use ManageHub to speed your business transformation project.

Chapter Two: Culture – How to win your employees' hearts, minds and cooperation by adopting an employee-centric culture.

Chapter Three: Process – How to engage your employees to document and improve the work they perform.

Chapter Four: Continuous Improvement – How to encourage your employees to share their ideas for improving your business.

Chapter Five: Coaching – How to establish an ongoing conversation with employees that sets expectations, mentors and supports their active participation.

Chapter Six: Team Meetings – How to hold your employees accountable for their commitments.

Chapter Two:
Reinvent Your Company Culture

An essential element of your business transformation initiative is to optimize your company's culture. Your company culture is its spiritual essence. It sets the standard for how people work together to achieve your company's mission.

Your company's culture is defined by its values. Values are like your company's moral code. Company values are usually defined by emotionally-charged words like:

- Integrity
- Loyalty
- Quality
- Innovation
- Passion
- Accountability
- Delighting customers
- Teamwork

Many organizations spend considerable time, effort, (and money) compiling their list of values. However, once identified, the exercise is often finished, filed, and forgotten. Leaders fail to translate their company-values into a set of expected employee behaviors.

ManageHub requires your company to adopt the following minimum set of basic, non-negotiable values-based behaviors:

- Promote consistent product/service quality and customer satisfaction.
- Actively document process knowhow.
- Share ideas and issues for improving the company.
- Participate in internal strategic projects (when needed).
- Actively learn new processes.
- Help coach, mentor and cross-train other employees in performing their processes
- Actively participate on process and collaboration-teams.

The above behaviors are designed to achieve key company values related to quality, innovation, teamwork, collaboration, continuous learning and continuous improvement. They also target the specific employee-behaviors that are required to bring your company's leadership framework to life. (The importance of each behavior is explained in more detail in subsequent chapters of this book.)

ManageHub Makes it Easy for Employees to Perform Their Expected "Non-Negotiable" Behaviors

ManageHub helps your employees perform your company's expected behaviors. All they need to do is log on to their ManageHub account to begin contributing knowledge and ideas and participating in improvement projects and collaboration conversations.

The following ManageHub tools and workspaces are particularly helpful in creating your company's tradition of ongoing employee engagement. However, keep in mind, your employees need your coaching and oversight to ensure that they are used.

- **Knowledgebase:** Encourage employees to use ManageHub's knowledgebase to document and improve process knowhow.
- **Suggestion System:** Encourage employees to use ManageHub's Communication Logs to share their ideas for improving quality, consistency, and customer satisfaction.
- **Project Management:** Encourage employees to use ManageHub's built in project management system to implement strategic improvement initiatives.
- **Employee Workspaces:** Use ManageHub's Employee Workspace to create an individual learning plan for every participant.
- **Process, Department and Group Workspaces:** Encourage employees to participate on multiple process and collaboration-teams.

Monitor the participation of individual employees by reviewing their dedicated ManageHub workspace. Every employee workspace lists all the activity generated by the related employee. The more knowledge they contribute, the more ideas they share, the more projects they manage… *the more valuable they are to your organization.*

Teach employees how to review their own workspaces to monitor their progress. Your objective is to help them become self-managed, self-motivated, and fully engaged participants.

Review the tabbed sections of an employee's workspace to assess their level of engagement. Use the workpace to structure an effective coaching conversation that encourages employees to contribute their knowledge, share their ideas, and participate in improvement projects.

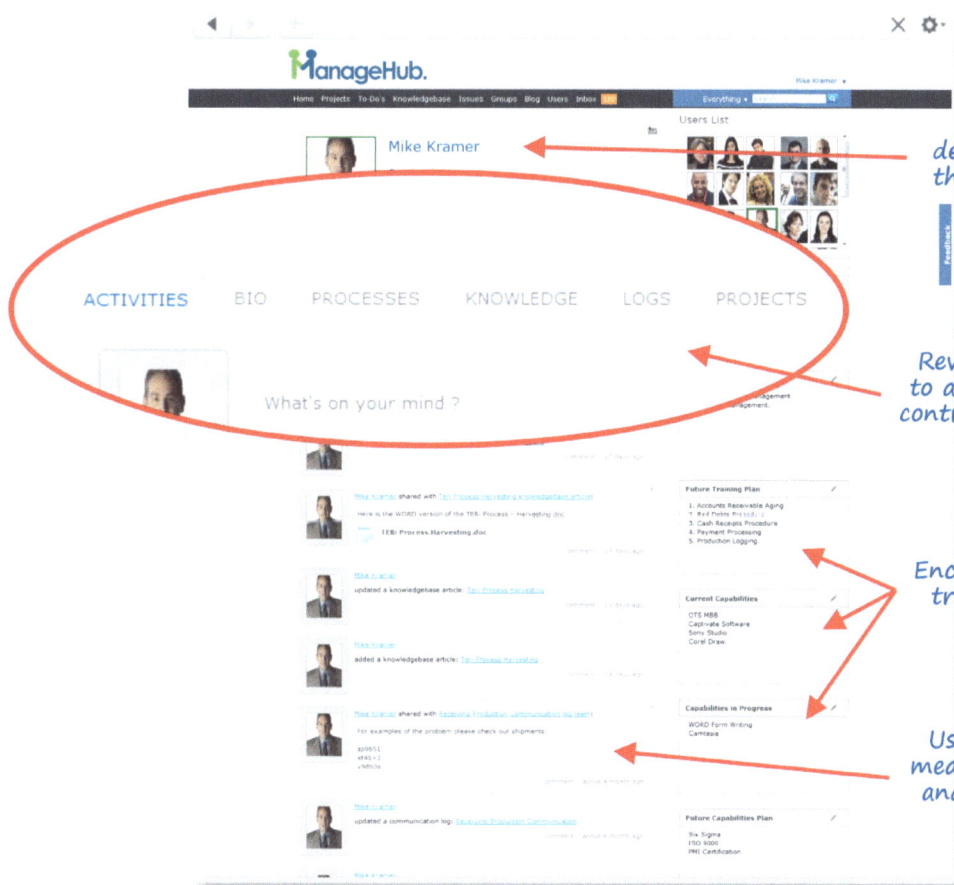

Every employee/user has a dedicated ManageHub workspace that automatically organizes and reports all of their activity.

Review tabbed workspace sections to assess the value of an employee's contributed knowledge, shared ideas, project participation, etc.

Encourage job-sharing and cross-training by creating a learning plan for every employee.

Use the workspace to structure meaningful coaching conversations and to create self-managed and self-motivated employees..

[19]

Your Role Leading Culture Change

For real culture change to occur *you* must adopt the right intentions. Your feelings and motivations set the tone for your company. Your business transformation initiative will fail if you do not live by your new values and principles. You need to demonstrate your personal commitment to quality, customer satisfaction and excellence. You must encourage, and when necessary, enforce use of your ManageHub framework. Your employees will be watching to see if your words have meaning.

Cultural transformation does not happen overnight. It takes time. You will need to constantly reinforce your reasons for adopting your company's new culture. Use one-on-one coaching and team meetings to discuss the benefits of each expected behavior. You will need to repeat your coaching conversations over and over again until your employee behaviors become second nature. (Both coaching and employee team meetings are discussed in later chapters of this book.)

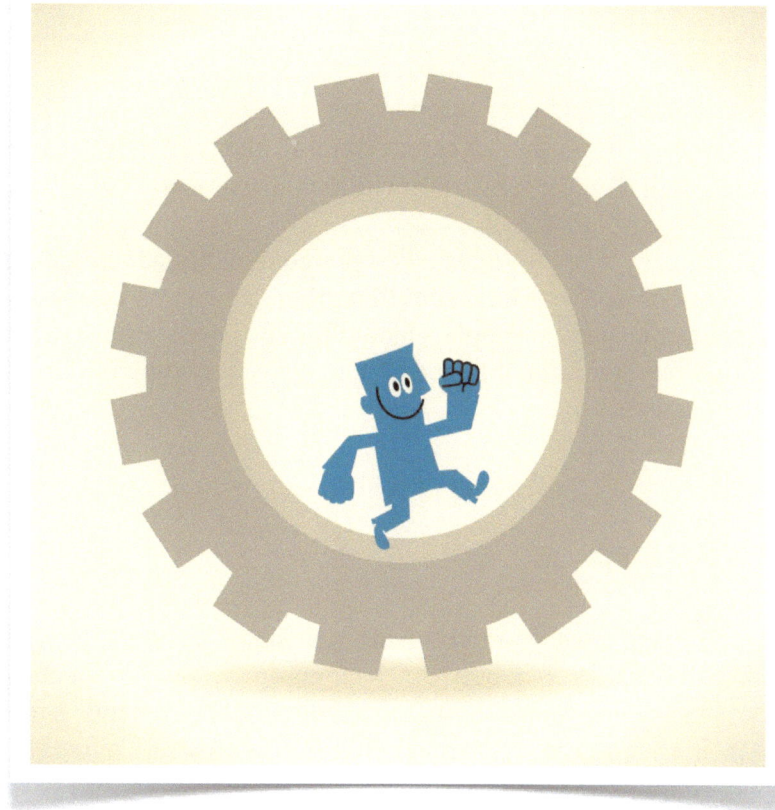

Chapter Three:
Systematize & Standardize Your Company's Processes

As you win your employees' hearts and minds, you will likely want to focus their attention on systematizing, standardizing and improving your company's day-to-day processes. The best way to do this is to organize your company into self-managed process-teams. Empowering your employees to manage the work they perform benefits your business on many levels:

- Encourages all employees to become active participants documenting and improving their areas of responsibility.
- Provides frontline employees with recognition, responsibility and prestige.
- Speeds the optimization of your company by spreading the responsibility to many people.
- Improves the accuracy and efficiency of your company's standardized procedures by having processes documented by the people who know them best.
- Helps eliminate bottlenecks and job traps.

- Teaches frontline employees important leadership skills.
- Supports policies of job sharing, cross training and continual learning.
- Enables promoting employees from within your company.

Optimizing your company's processes is a key prerequisite to breaking through to its next level of success. Your objective is to ensure that processes can be performed consistently and are not dependent on specific people, (including you), preforming specific work. This makes your company resilient, flexible and able to grow quickly without sacrificing quality or customer satisfaction.

Business Model Map

A good starting point is to create your company's Business Model Map. A Business Model Map depicts the relationship between your company's departments, processes and employees. Processes are associated with their managing departments. Employees are associated with their assigned process areas. This simple structure allows you and your employees to understand how your business operates.

Your company's Business Model Map provides many advantages over a traditional Organizational Chart. Org-charts represent the spiritual foundations of most dysfunctional cultures. They focus on job-titles instead of process-areas. They emphasize lines of authority over personal responsibility. They favor middle-managers at the expense of frontline employees. They encourage anti-social behaviors like managing upwards, power grabbing, politicking, and maneuvering for greater influence. They institutionalize information filtering which makes it difficult for frontline employees to freely communicate their valuable ideas for improving your company. They cannot be used as a tactical, strategic tool.

On the other hand, your Business Model Maps favors a flat organizational hierarchy. It focuses on processes not job-titles. It empowers frontline employees to manage and improve their own areas of responsibility. It provides the insights you need to configure your departments, processes and employees to achieve optimal performance. It is also a valuable strategic planning tool that helps you identify operational gaps, and creates an aligned set of department and process improvement objectives.

Your company's Business Model Map uses the following simple outline structure to depict the relationships between departments, processes and employees:

- Example Department 1
    - Example Process-Team A
        - Employee (Manager)
        - Employee (Staff)
    - Example Process-Team B
        - Employee (Manager)

- Employee (Staff)

Departments: The purpose of a department is to categorize related work activities. Categorizing related work activities makes them easier to manage. For example, most startup companies do not have many processes to manage. As a result, they typically have a very simple department structure. As a company grows, the number of process areas explode. Owners and employees begin to naturally organize related processes into departments. The typical textbook-set of departments include:

- Finance/Accounting
- Sales & Marketing Department
- Human Resources (HR)
- Information Technology (IT)
- Research & Development (R and D)
- Customer Service Department
- Operations Department

The above text-book department names are often too formal for smaller companies. A better approach is to choose names that you and your employees casually use to refer to your departments. This helps make your Business Model Map feel real. For example a medical facility may have department names like Clinical, Lab, and Billing. A manufacturing company may have department names like Engineering, Machine Shop, Quality Control, and Warehouse.

Processes: The definition of the word "process" is often a source of confusion. A process is an individual work activity. Processes *are not* job-titles or job-descriptions. They answer the question, "What do you do at work?" Each process should relate to only one delegable job role. Each process name should include a verb (action word.) Examples of processes include:

- Reconcile bank statements
- Input daily raw material cost updates
- Produce monthly customer newsletter
- Conduct new employee orientation
- Perform monthly software updates
- Change air conditioner filters.

Process Team: Once your processes are organized into departments, you need to identify the employees who perform them. Employees generally serve on multiple process teams. This is especially true in smaller companies where every employee is expected to wear multiple hats. Designate one employee to serve as manager for each process. Choose the employee who is the most knowledgeable and experienced in performing the process.

Download Your Business Model Map Template: Use the following spreadsheet template to create your company's Business Model Map. The spreadsheet helps you keep track of which processes are optimized. It also doubles as a valuable strategic planning tool.

A Business Model Map spreadsheet template can be downloaded from our information website at www.ManageHub.info/downloads.

Use the first row of the spreadsheet to indicate your company's mission and vision. Then set up the spreadsheet with the following column headings:

- Department
- Process
- Manager/Staff
- Systematized (using software, checklists, machinery, etc)
- Standardized (with step-by-step operating procedures, or video.)
- Bottleneck?
- Strategic/Improvement Objectives

Complete the spreadsheet by identifying all of your company's departments and related processes. Indicate the names of the process managers and team members associated with every process. Indicate if the process is systematized, standardized, or is a bottleneck by placing an "X" in the appropriate column(s). Also, indicate one or more strategic improvement objectives related to each department and process. When completed, your Business Model Map is a powerful management tool. Use your Business Model Map to:

- Set up your ManageHub organizational structure.
- Assign responsibility to frontline employees.
- Identify operational gaps that need to be filled.
- Configure your business for maximum efficiency.

[24]

- Help your employees understand how all the moving parts of your company work together and how they fit into the bigger picture.
- Communicate your company's strategic plan.
- Review your company, department and process objectives and to make sure they are complementary and aligned.

Share your Business Model Map with your employees. Use it to engage them in an ongoing dialogue. Use it to gather their insights and to make better strategic decisions.

Use Your Business Model Map to Setup ManageHub

Your Business Model map is a handy reference when setting up your ManageHub leadership framework. It neatly organizes all of your company's departments, processes, and people in exactly the format you need to speed setup.

Step One: Complete your Business Model Map.

Step Two: Log on to your ManageHub Account.

Step Three: Click on the related icon 🔧, ⚙, or 👤 to create a ManageHub workspace for every department, process, and user indicated on your Business Model Map worksheet.

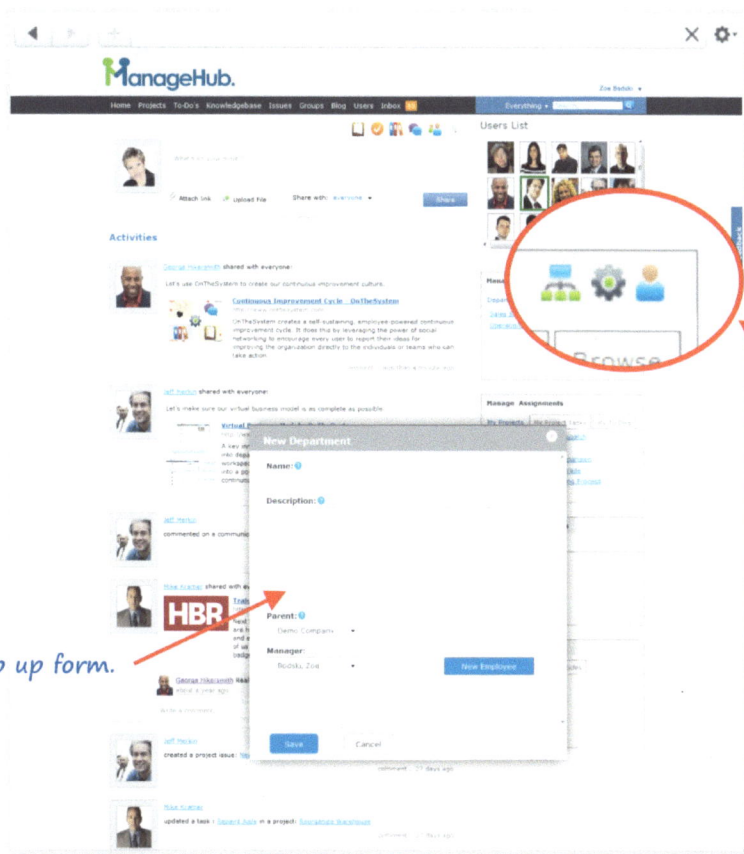

Create a Department

Create a Process

Create a User

Complete the pop up form.

Step Four: Complete the popup set up form. Once saved, your department, process, or user, will appear in the related tabbed section of your link box. (Some browsers may require you to refresh your screen before the link will appear.

Step Five: Repeat Steps Three and Four until your entire business model structure is created.

To view your organizational-structure report, click on the full-screen icon 🖳 located in the "Browse" section of the "ManageHubs" link box.

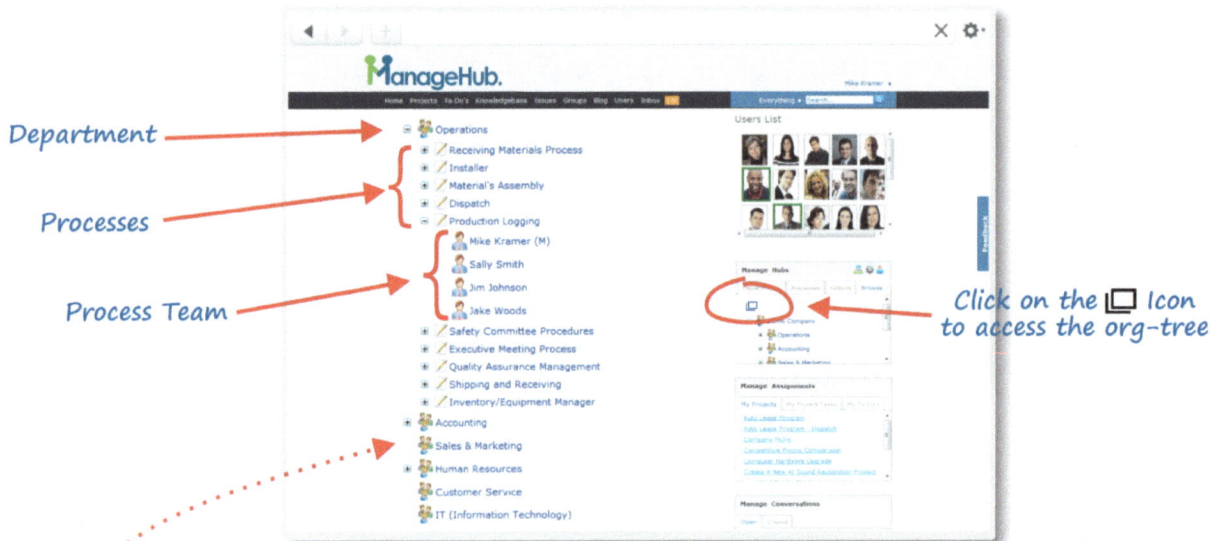

Department

Processes

Process Team

Click on the 🖳 Icon to access the org-tree

Every organizational element in the list is a clickable link that takes you to a unique workspace where you can manage all of the projects, ideas, problems, discussions, and knowledge that are related to the selected department, process, or employee.

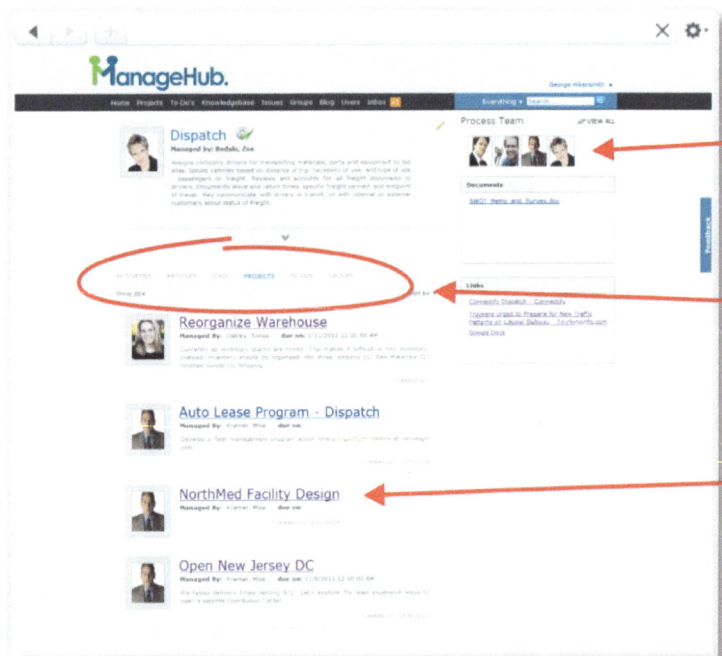

The Facegrid identifies all of the people associated with the workspace.

Tabbed workspace sections keep you very organized.

Clickable links take you to related workspaces.

Process Management Worksheet

So far, you should have completed your Business Model Map and set up your ManageHub department, process, and user workspaces. Next, create one Process Management Worksheet for every process identified on your Business Model Map.

Use the Process Management Worksheets to:

- Teach employees how to be effective process managers and team participants. (In smaller companies it is likely that most employees will serve both roles.)
- Encourage employees to adopt your company's values-based behaviors.
- Populate your ManageHub process-team workspaces.

To complete the Process Management Worksheet, indicate the process name, department, manager name and team members. Next, indicate a process description and improvement objective. Then record all issues and problems that have been reported to the process team. The source of these issues can be the process team, the employee-survey or ManageHub Communication Logs. (The survey and ComLogs are discussed in the next chapter.) Also, use the worksheet to indicate any related improvement projects created to resolve reported issues.

Process Management Worksheet

Process Name	Reconcile Bank Statements
Department	Accounting
Process Manager	Fred Palmer
Process Team	Jamie Rader
	Jeff Zimmer
	Fred Palmer

ManageHub.
for the BreakthroughProject.com

Process Description

Reconciling our bank statements is a process that allows our company to know exactly how much money we have and to ensure that there are no errors on the part of our bank or ourselves. We verify deposits, withdrawals, checks and payments. Errors may arise from forgetting to enter a check, payment or withdrawal.

Process Objective

Have all bank reconciliations complete by the 7th of each month.

Switchboard Issue	Record Project/Resolution
We can save about 6 hours of work a month if we could integrate our accounting program with our bank.	

Standardization Checklist

How is the process systematized? (Software? Checklists? Lot Sheets?)	Software, standard work-paper
Do you have step-by-step procedures? (Written, Video or both)	Written instructions
Are your procedures good enough to support independent learning?	Yes
Are you supporting cross-training or job-sharing?	We are cross-training two warehouse employees who want to learn accounting.
Is your process a current or potential bottleneck?	No
Are all the members of your team actively helping document and improve the process?	Yes. We are all helping cross train the warehouse staff. We are learning ways to streamline the process.

The Process Management Worksheet is a valuable teaching tool. Use it to train process managers to be good *managers.* Use it to set expectations and focus your process team's effort on achieving the following key objectives:

- **Systematization:** The process is automated using software, checklists, lot sheets, etc.
- **Standardization:** The process is documented with step-by-step procedures.
- **Training Methods:** The process procedures are good enough to support independent learning.
- **Cross-Training/Job-Sharing:** The process team is actively training multiple employees.
- **Bottleneck:** The process team is ensuring the process is not a current or future bottleneck.
- **Employee Engagement:** All process team members are actively helping document and improve the process.

A Process Management Worksheet can be downloaded from our information website at www.ManageHub.info/downloads.

Use Your Process Management Worksheets to Populate ManageHub Process Workspaces

ManageHub Process Workspaces automate process-team collaboration. They make it easy for you to monitor your teams' progress and hold them accountable for documenting and improving their areas of responsibility. They also help structure meaningful coaching conversations and team meetings.

Every workspace includes a dedicated activity feed that provides you with a chronological change-history. Tabbed sections organize all related knowledge, projects, and Communication Log discussions.

Populate your ManageHub process workspaces by referring to your Process Management Worksheets:

Step One (Optional): Complete one Process Management Worksheet for every process identified on you company's Business Model Map. The worksheets are a handy source-document that speeds setup.

Step Two: Click on the ⚙ icon, located at the top of your ManageHub link box on your home page, to create one management workspace for every process. (Skip this step if the process was already created.)

Step Three (If needed): Click on the ✏ icon to add or edit the process name, manager, managing department, process description, strategic objective, or to approve new members.

Step Four: Refer to your Process Management Worksheets to populate each process workspace with all the 📚 knowledge (policies, procedures, training methods), 📋 improvement projects, 💬 ideas, and problems related to each process. Click on the ➕ icon located at the top of each tabbed section to add content.

Step Five: Manage the process by monitoring the workspace's activity-feed and reviewing the tabbed workspace sections. Make sure your process teams are actively engaged systematizing, standardizing, and improving their processes. If they are not collaborating successfully, you will need to increase the frequency of one-on-one coaching and team meetings.

ManageHub Process Workspaces automate process-team collaboration.
They make it easy for you to monitor your teams' progress and hold
them accountable for documenting and improving their areas of responsibility.
They also help structure meaningful coaching conversations and team meetings.

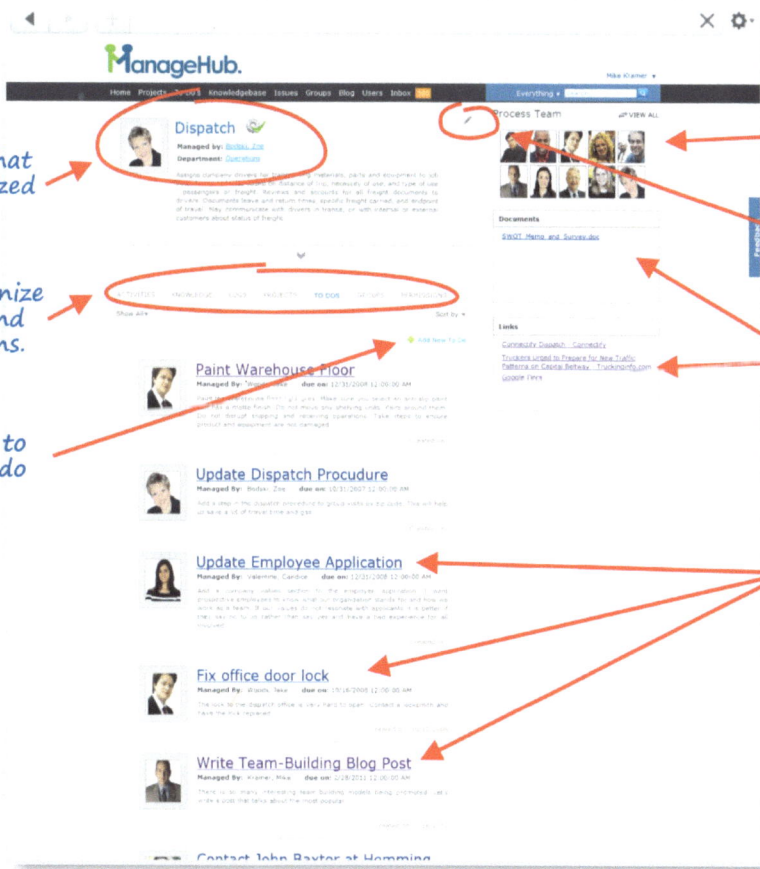

The icon ✅ indicates that the process is systematized and standardized.

Workspace sections organize knowledge, projects, and improvement discussions.

Click the ➕ icon to create a new to-do assignmnent.

The Facegrid identifies your process-team.

Click on the ✏ icon to edit the workspace.

Link boxes provide easy access to shared documents and files.

Clickable links take you to related workspaces.

Use ManageHub Process Workspaces to Structure Coaching Conversations and Team Meetings

Perform a systematic review of a ManageHub process workspace including its header and tabbed sections to guide a consistent coaching conversation or team meeting.

- **Process Header:** Review the process description and objective (located under the header pull down.) Make sure process team members understand them. Ask members if they can be improved? Show members how they can click on the "Suggest" link provided to report an idea for improving the process's strategic improvement objective."

- **Process Facegrid:** Review the workspace's facegrid. Are all the members actively participating on your process team? Are they functioning as a collaboration community? If not, they require additional coaching, training, and monitoring. Does the process team include enough members to avoid current or potential bottlenecks? Is the process team actively recruiting and training new members?

- **Knowledge Tab:** Review the knowledgebase entries associated with the process workspace. Do they include all of the policies, step-by-step procedures, training methods, videos, schematics, flowcharts, or any other information that helps define the process's current standard of excellence? Are the listed knowledgebase entries sufficient to train a new process-team member with a minimum of direct support? Remind process team members that your company's objective is to minimize "job traps" that prevent promoting from within. If members resist sharing their knowledge, remind them that if they are not *replaceable, they are not promotable.* Be sure to acknowledge and praise members who contributed valuable new knowledge.

- **Issues Tab:** Review the issues associated with the process workspace. Is each issue being actively discussed? If not, ask team members, (individually, or as a group), if they have any insights or solutions to contribute to the listed ComLog workspaces. Determine if any of the issues should be marked as resolved. Determine if any of the issues should be converted into a project or To-Do assignment. Are there any important newly posted issues that should be discussed? Ask participants if they have any ideas or issues that they have not shared. If they have ideas, have them create the ComLog using their logon credentials so that they receive proper credit. Remind participants that ComLogs fuel your company's continuous improvement cycle. Be sure to acknowledge and praise members who contributed valuable new ideas and/or issues.

- **Projects Tab:** Review the projects associated with each process workspace. Are the projects meeting their task due-dates? Are the projects on budget? Are all process-team members participating on, or managing, one or more projects? Ask project managers to report on their progress by reviewing the header and tabbed sections of the project's workspace. Are there any project issues that need resolution? Remind process team members that managing improvement projects helps them develop critical leadership skills that prepare them for promotion. Be sure to acknowledge and praise members who participate on successful improvement projects.

- **To-Do Tab:** To-Dos are one-task assignments. They are a great way to keep track of one-off tasks assigned to individual team members during meetings. Review the To-Dos associated with the process workspace. Ask To-Do managers to report on their progress. Be sure to acknowledge and praise members who successfully completed their assigned To-Do assignments.

- **Groups Tab:** Groups are collaboration workspaces. They can be used to manage Special Interest Groups (SIGs), client engagements, cross-department or cross-organizational collaboration. Groups can be associated with a process team workspace. This can be useful when the process team is responsible for managing the group's collaboration. The Group workspace can be populated with knowledgebase entries, ComLogs, projects, to-do's, and uploaded documents, and links. Group members are either invited or are approved. It is sometimes helpful to review a Group's activity during a coaching conversation or a team meeting. However, keep in mind that many Groups are private. This means that their activity is not known to all participants.

Process Managers Role & Responsibilities

Assign the senior-most knowledge holder to be the Process Manager. Process Managers are responsible for engaging their teams to optimize their assigned work activity.

The Process Manager has three primary responsibilities:

1. **Systematizing, standardizing and documenting the process.** This includes creating and updating the process's policies, procedures, training methods, forms, checklists and other documents.
2. **Managing the process's continual improvement cycle.** This includes responding to the ideas, suggestions and feedback communicated via your ManageHub Communication Logs. (ComLogs are discussed in Chapter Four.)
3. **Managing process team collaboration and participation.** When possible, the manager's objective is to create a team of three or more employees who are cross trained and actively engaged in helping to improve the process.

You should treat Process Managers as the most valued and honored position in your company. They represent the future leaders of your company. They serve as frontline ambassadors for creating your company's culture of excellence. Acknowledge their hard work. Have them report on their progress during your company's regular team accountability meetings using their ManageHub process workspace to structure their presentation.

Make sure your Process Managers understand that efficient and effective processes are the key to making your company more scalable and better prepared for rapid growth. Reinforce that your objective is to reduce your company's dependence on specific employees performing specific work. Explain that optimizing your company's processes benefits your employees by eliminating their job traps, and freeing them for promotion. Explain that you want to create generations of leaders who can grow with your growing company.

Provide your Process Managers (and teams) with the professional support they need to be successful. Hire outside resources when necessary. Your objective is to create a highly engaged group of dependable, loyal and aligned frontline employees who will help you systematize, standardize and continuously improve your company, one process at a time. The more employees you can engage as Process Managers, and on process teams, the faster you can optimize and transform you company.

Systematize Every Process

A primary responsibility of every process team is to systematize and standardize the work-activity that they manage.

To systematize a process means it is automated or controlled by software, machinery, lot sheets, checklists, forms or some other structured approach. The purpose of systematizing a process is to minimize the variation in its performance so that common errors and mistakes do not occur.

It is also important that quality assurance be built into every system. This means that the process is tracked and audited as it is being performed. This helps confirm that mistakes and defects do not creep into your automated process. If a problem does occur, the system should include provisions for reporting and resolving the issue so that it does not recur.

Forms and checklists are often an inexpensive and effective way to systematize a process. They add structure and guide your employee's performance of repetitive tasks. They provide a completeness check that reminds employees to perform key steps that could be missed. They also provide an important source-document for future review. When a problem or error occurs, you can easily modify the form, add a step, or add an audit point to ensure that the issue does not recur in the future.

A word of caution: Some employees will perceive the concept of "systems" negatively. They incorrectly believe that systems are too structured, or will stifle their creativity. The opposite is true. Effective systems help improve the creative-dynamic in your company. Instead of experiencing the constant stress and aggravation of spinning their wheels and putting out the same fires, your systems help ensure that the fires never start. The structure of your systems frees everyone's time to focus on innovating, creating, improving and building your company.

Standardize Every Process

To standardize a process means it is documented with step-by-step operating procedures. The procedures should be so clear and complete that they ensure the process can be performed consistently, and without mistakes, by any qualified, well-trained and approved employee.

The purpose of standardizing your processes is to establish your company's current benchmark of excellence. Well documented processes represent your company's internal best practices that all employees are expected to adopt. They should work hand-in-hand with related automated systems to reduce variation in the way the process is performed. The more your company can reduce the variation in the way its processes are performed, the more your employees can increase consistency, productivity, and overall quality.

SOPs and PALs: Many organizations create a formal set of Standardized Operating Procedures (SOPs). These procedures are usually bound in a set of binders, or are stored electronically in a folder on their company's hard drive. Some quality-professionals refer to these procedure-sets as a Process Asset Library (PAL).

SOPs or PALs are created for all the right reasons. Leaders realize the value of documenting the know-how of operating their companies. However, the problem is that most standardization projects are treated as periodic exercises. Improvement is not built-in. As a result, organizational flexibility and innovation is not achieved.

ManageHub improves upon the typical process standardization approach by providing your company with a *collaborative* PAL. It works by organizing your company into process teams. Every process team is provided with a dedicated online workspace where members can work together to standardize and improve their process.

Your objective in using ManageHub should be to transform process standardization and improvement from a periodic exercise into an ongoing, living activity. When performed correctly, the benefits should extend well beyond creating a set of neatly organized processes. Your company should experience:

- Increased product/service quality and consistency (even in geographically distributed teams because all related employees are members of the process team and agree on applying the same standard-of-practice.)
- Improved productivity.
- Significant cost savings.
- Increased innovation.
- Increased customer satisfaction.

[33]

- Increased organizational flexibility, resilience and responsiveness.
- Engaged employee who know what is expected of them.
- Employees who know how to lead.

The screenshots on the next page explain how process-team workspaces are organized into department managed PALs.

Every department in your company can manage its own Process Asset Library (PAL). Access the library by clicking on the Process Tab in the Department's workspace. Then click on any process name to review the related process team workspace.

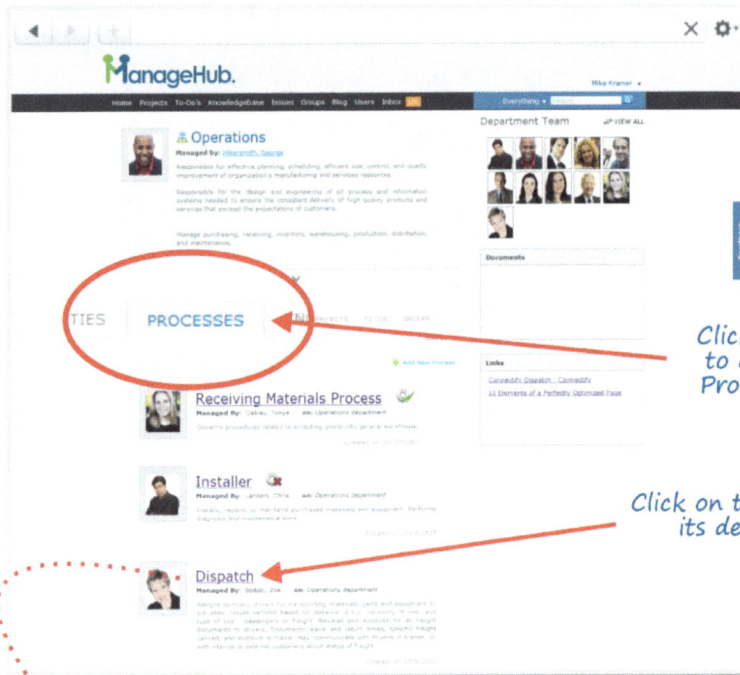

Click on the "Processes" tab to access the department's Process Asset Library (PAL) link list.

Click on the process's ink to access its dedicated collaboration workspace.

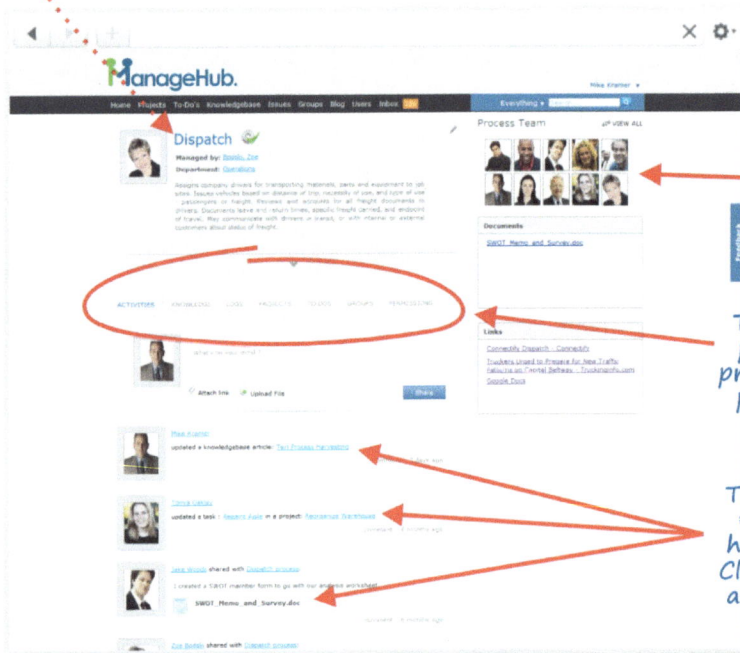

The Facegrid identifies your process team.

Tabbed workspace sections provide quick access to all process knowledge, ComLogs, projects, assignments, etc.

The activity feed provides you with a chronological change history related to the process. Click on any link to drill-down and review the changed item.

Engage your process-teams: Documenting most of your company's processes should be quite easy. In addition to written, step-by-step procedures, teams can upload screen capture videos to the ManageHub knowledgebase and associate them with their process workspace. Videos are a great way to explain how to perform step-by-step procedures like completing an online data entry form. Employees can use a smart phone to record a video of an employee performing the process. They can include the relevant pages from a software manual. They should include anything and everything that makes it easy to train an employee to perform the process with a minimum of hand-holding.

Hire an experienced business coach or process consultant to help guide, monitor or support teams who are managing complex, critical or broken processes.

Remind employees that process documentation and improvement is not an occasional exercise that is finished, filed and forgotten. It is an ongoing, continuous journey that is never completed. It usually takes three or more iterations for the process documentation to come into clear focus.

Once the documentation is effective, it should become the benchmark for performing the process. Anytime a problem, waste or inefficiency creeps into the process, the team should report the issue using your ManageHub Communication Logs 💬. ComLogs make it easy for your employees to discuss ways to modify their systems and procedures to eliminate the possibility of the issue recurring in the future. This active engagement by process teams becomes the cornerstone of your company's continuous improvement quality culture. (Using ManageHub to automate your company's continuous improvement cycle is discussed in the next chapter.)

Process Standardization Format: In larger organizations, standardized procedures are often formal documents that are supported by related schematics, process flowcharts, training materials, and/or other reference materials. Although this type of detail may not be necessary in your business, it is a good idea to standardize the way your process teams *standardize*. You can do this by adopting a company-wide standardization template that all process teams use to format their step-by-step procedures. Adopting a standardized format makes it easier for employees to cross train in multiple roles. It also helps prepare your company for quality certifications like ISO 9000®. *A Standardization Format can be downloaded from our information website at* www.ManageHub.info/downloads.

ManageHub Knowledgebase: ManageHub includes a collaborative knowledge management system to speed your company's standardization project. The ManageHub knowledgebase features a built in word processor to capture, store, and continuously update your organization's valuable know-how. You can also upload a document or attach a link to a file stored on an external, cloud-based source. Use the ManageHub Knowledgebase to organize your process's policies, procedures and training methods. Also, use it to store any other company related documents like meeting minutes and client related files.

To create a new knowledge entry, simple click on the 📚 link on your home page.

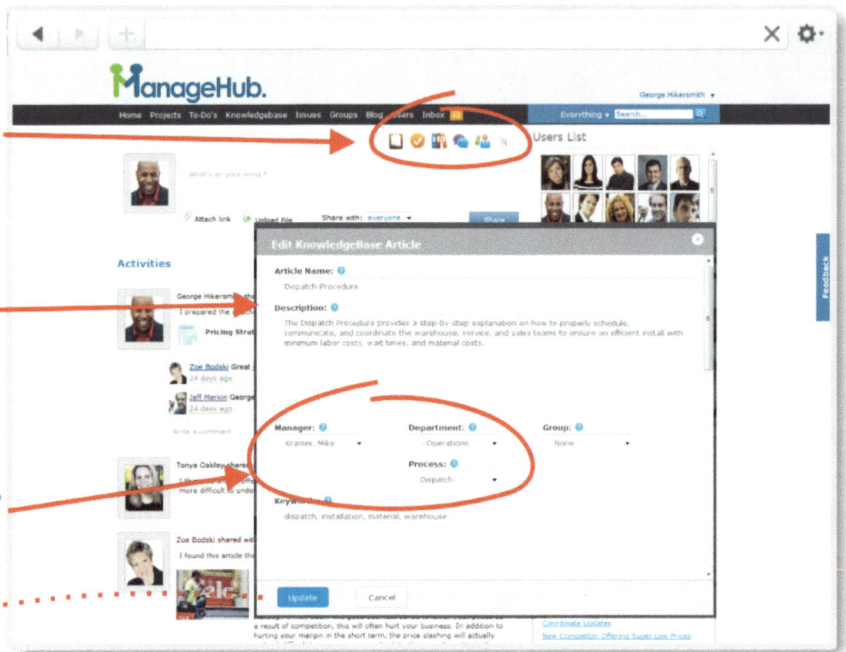

Click on the 📚 icon to contribute knowledge.

Complete the pop-up data entry window.

Assigning your knowledge to a Manager, Department, and Process-Team to alert the right people to your new information.

Save your entry to create a knowledgebase workspace where you and invited participants can collaborate using the built-in text editor, attach documents, share links, and discuss ideas.

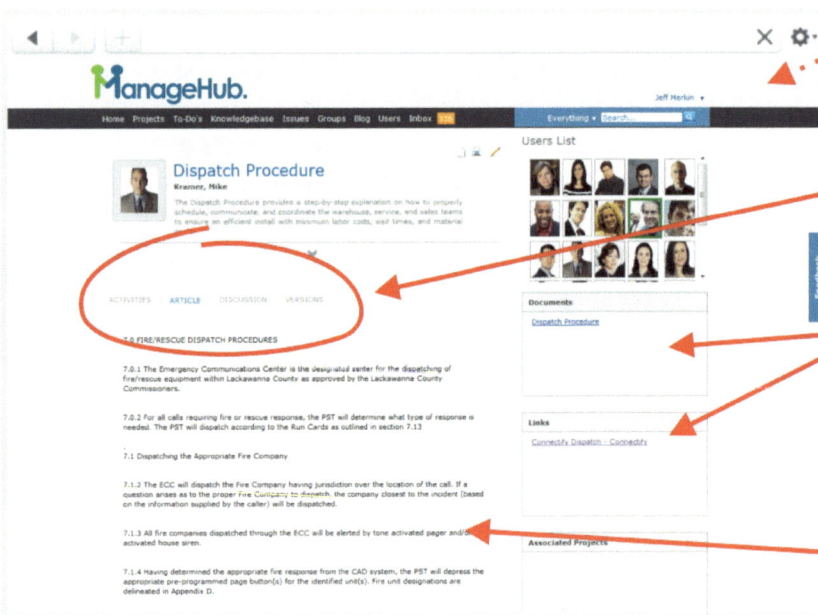

Tabbed workspace sections keep you very organized.

Link boxes provide you with handy access to attached documents, and external links.

Use the built-in text editor to compose a policy, procedure, training plan, or other information.

ManageHub Projects: ManageHub includes an interactive project management system that is designed to manage internal, strategic improvement initiatives. However, you can use it to manage external or client projects too. The system features a built-in issues resolution engine that project participants can use to identify and resolve project related problems. The system also includes automated email alerts with reply back capabilities. You can even duplicate existing projects to speed the setup of recurring initiatives.

To create a project, click on the [ ] icon on your home screen. You can also create a project by clicking on the [+] icon that is located at the top of the "Projects" tab of all ManageHub workspaces. Then complete the pop up setup screen. Be sure to use the drop down list to associate your new project with its managing Department, Process, and/or Group. Once created, a link to the project will appear on all related Department, Process and/or Group workspaces. Among the first projects you should create are process systemization and standardization initiatives. Consider creating one project to manage the optimization of every process.

Easy edit icons and slide down panels reveal project details.

Tabbed workspace sections keep your project organized.

Drag and drop task lists with cool click and slide animation.

Click on the "show more" icon and all the task's information will slide into view.

Every project workspace has its own built-in issues resolution system
where team-members can report and resolve project related problems.
To access the project's issues click on the "Issues" tab.

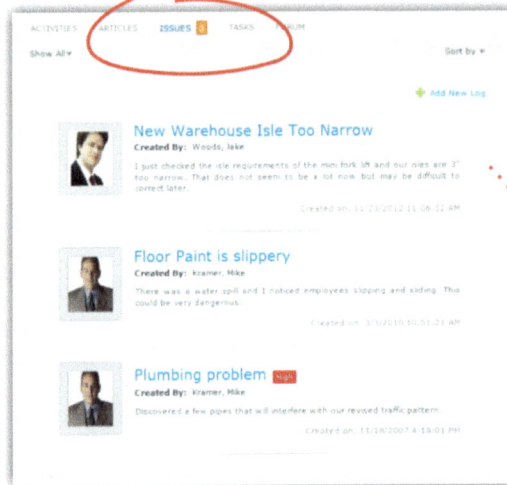

A conversation workspace will slide into view
where the project-team can discuss and
resolve the issue without emails or meetings.

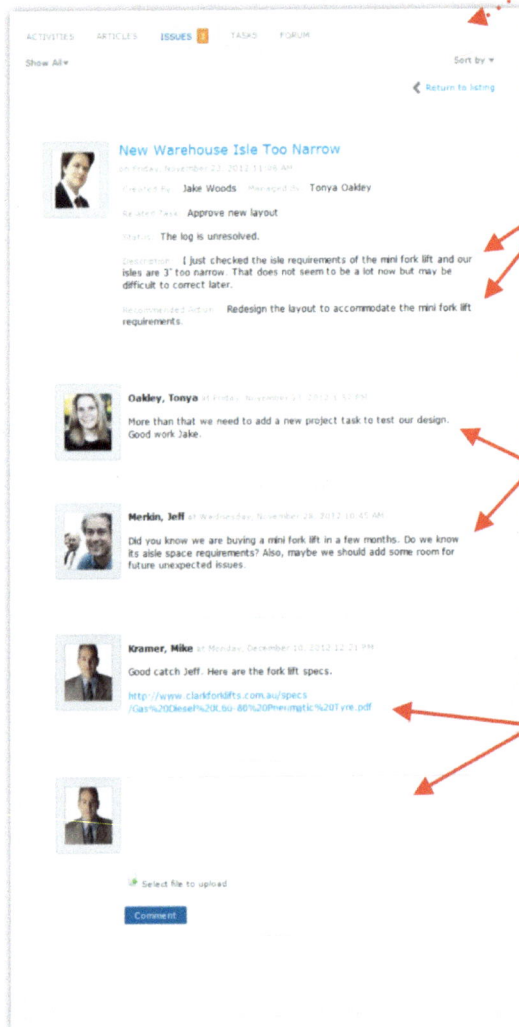

The issue header
defines the problem,
assigns responsibility,
and recommends a
solution.

Managing your team's
conversation in one place
reduces email, and minimize
the need for meetings.

ManageHub makes
it easy to share comments,
links, and files.

A Strategy for Startups and Solo-Entrepreneurs: If you manage a very small company or are a solo-entrepreneur, you will likely need to serve as Process Manager for most, if not all, of your processes. Systematizing, standardizing and improving so many processes may require many late nights that test your commitment and determination. However, do not be discouraged. Start by completing your Business Model Map and setting up your department and process workspaces on ManageHub. Seeing the big picture will help you stay focused and prioritize a list of processes that you will optimize first.

Start by systematizing and standardizing processes you would like to immediately delegate to part-time employees or virtual assistants. Next, tackle elements of your day-to-day operations that do not require your direct involvement, creativity, or expertise. Finally, develop systems and standards that allow you delegate more and more of your work to well trained and supervised employees. Your goal should be to create a set of processes that allows your daily work to be performed by employees (or contractors), and you to serve in more of an oversight and quality-control role. This helps prepare your business for rapid growth, unexpected opportunities, and unforeseen events, like a personal health crisis. It also helps prepare your business for eventual sale. After all, the value of your business is diminished when it is overly dependent on you or a key employee.

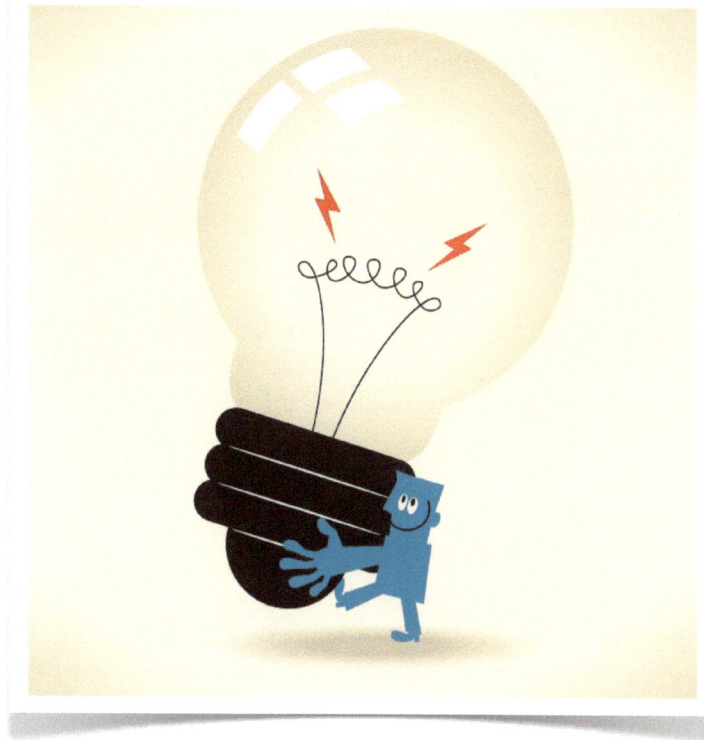

Chapter Four:
Use ComLogs to Create Employee-Powered Continuous Improvement

The third required element in designing your company's business transformation is to initiate an ongoing continuous improvement cycle. This requires you to open direct lines of communication between your employees and your company's process teams. You want to create a culture where employees feel comfortable sharing ideas, suggestions and problems directly with relevant process teams. You also want to empower process teams to vet and resolve the issues related to their areas of responsibility and expertise. Your objective is to fully leverage the knowledge, ideas and insights of your employees to improve product quality, consistency, customer satisfaction and eliminate waste. Empowering employees to drive the right information to the right people helps create a highly flexible organization that is able to outmaneuver its competition.

Your role is to keep the continuous improvement momentum going:

- Encourage employees to report their ideas.

- Use ManageHub to monitor significant issues from the moment they are reported to their resolution.
- Facilitate collaboration when needed.
- Credit and reward employees for contributing their good ideas.
- Credit and reward process-teams that take quick and effective action to resolve issues.

Managing communication is the key to ensuring that a steady stream of employee ideas fuels your company's continuous improvement cycle. A company-wide survey helps start the cycle. ManageHub's Communication Logs (ComLogs) keeps it going.

Company-Wide Survey & Analysis

Your Company's continuous improvement cycle needs a starting point. It is often helpful to begin with a company-wide survey. Use the survey to identify all of the recurring problems, concerns, snafus, complaints, and inefficiencies that impact the growth, innovation, and customer satisfaction of your business. It is like a company-wide data-dump.

CEO - Tom Smith	VP - Jane Adams	VP - Lev Linquist	VP - Sue Smith	VP - Jan Murphy	Problem/Threat	Idea/Op	Other			Issue Description	Priority	Purchaseing Circle	ManageHub	Daily Store Management Log	Project
										Merchandizing / Purchasing					
x	x				x			6	1	Purchase wrong sytles	2			x	Subscribe to trend reports. Attend trade shows.
x		x	x	x	x			1	2	Purchase wrong sizes	2	x			
					x			1	3	Vendor relations/loyalty attached to employee not store	1	x			
x					x			3	4	Over order or Under order	2	x			
	x				x			2	5	Only one person knows how to purchase	1		x		
					x				6	Create a new baby center	2				Create a ManageHub project
									7						
										Retail Space Operations					
x	x				x			5	1	Operations are disorganized. Everyone does own thing	1	x			
					x			2	2	floors are not clean	1		x		
	x				x			1	3	Racks are not sized/straightened	1		x		
					x			1	4	Scheduling is unfair	2				Purchase scheduling software that accounts for employee type.
		x			x			9	5	Scheduling does not ensure experts are on the floor at all tim	2				
x					x			2	6	Restocking retruns and changing rooms is slow	1		x		
					x			7	7	All stores should look and work the same	5		x		make a long term strategy. Use Managehub to align all stores processes.
										Employees					
		x			x			2	1	Hiring people who do not relate to customer	1				Create Interview checklist and format that emphasizes behaviors, skills, personality (DISC)
					x			3	2	Some employees don't care about the store	1	x			Coaching
x					x			2	3	Conflicts simmer...are not resoved. Too much politicking	1	x			Coaching
x					x			4	4	No one shares their ideas.	1	x			Coaching
	x				x			4	5	No one listens to their ideas.	1	x			Coaching
					x			9	6	Managers play favorites	1	x			Coaching
x					x			3	7	No team spirit		x			Coaching
										Category 4					
									1						
									2						

Sheet1 / Sheet2 / Sheet3

In addition to operational issues, you should also identify the leadership, management and organizational issues that negatively impact your business.

A "Memo Template," Employee Survey," "Analysis Worksheet" and "Process Management Worksheet" are downloadable from our information website at www.ManageHub.info/downloads.

- The **"Memo Template"** explains the purpose of the survey to your employees and provides instructions. Customize it to serve the needs of your company.
- The **"Employee Survey Template"** asks your employees to identify opportunities for saving money, making money, operating more efficiently, resolving problems and growing sales.
- The **"Analysis Worksheet"** (shown above) helps you aggregate, categorize, prioritize and report survey responses.

Instead of sending a formal, written survey, you can use the "Employee Survey Template" to structure face-to-face employee interviews. Ask your employees what recurring customer complaints frustrate them? Ask what operational problems result in waste, inefficiency and avoidable expense? Ask what cultural, leadership and employee issues create a drag on growth, quality and innovation?

When analyzing your list of issues, you will likely be surprised by the quantity and consistency of your employee's ideas and suggestions. Notice that the value of the reported issues grows the closer you come to your front-lines. Keep track of which employees complete their survey thoughtfully and enthusiastically. These employees will likely lend significant support to your ManageHub business transformation initiative. Conversely, you will need to carefully manage those who resist or complain.

Your completed "Analysis Worksheet" provides you with a master list of open issues and a prioritized list of improvement projects. Create a separate 💬 Communication Log to track each individual open issue. Also, create a separate ManageHub 📙 project to manage each improvement initiative.

ManageHub Communication Logs (ComLogs)

Your company-wide employee survey is a one-time exercise that opens the flood gates of your employee's pent up ideas and operational problems. Use it as a catalyst to jumpstart your company's new continuous improvement cycle. Once completed, use your ManageHub Communication Logs to keep the cycle going.

Communication Logs are like an online suggestion box for your company. They empower every employee with the ability to share their ideas for improving your organization directly with the people who are most likely able to take quick action. With one click on the 💬 icon on their ManageHub home screen, a user can report a customer complaint, suggest a way to reduce waste, improve productivity, increase quality, open a new market, report competitive intelligence, or share an innovative idea. Once reported, your entire organization can work together to resolve the issue.

[43]

Encourage your employees to use Communication Logs (ComLogs) to share their ideas, and to report and resolve problems. Every ComLog has its own dedicated meeting room where participants can discuss the issue. They can attach document and share links. Use ComLogs instead of email, conference calls, and face-to-face meetings.

Click on the 💬 icon to start a discussion, or report an issue.

Complete the pop-up data entry window.

Assigning your issue to a Manager, Department, and Process-Team to alert the right people.

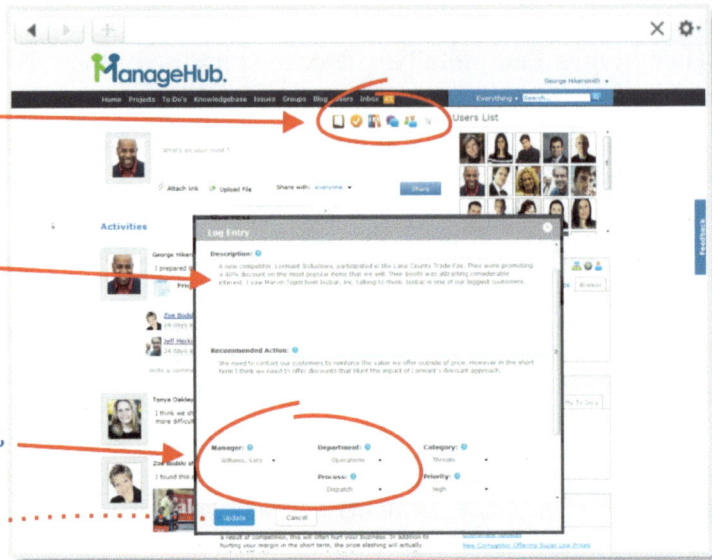

Save your issue to create a wonderful communication workspace where participants can work to resolve the issue without the usual meetings, email, interruptions, and distractions.

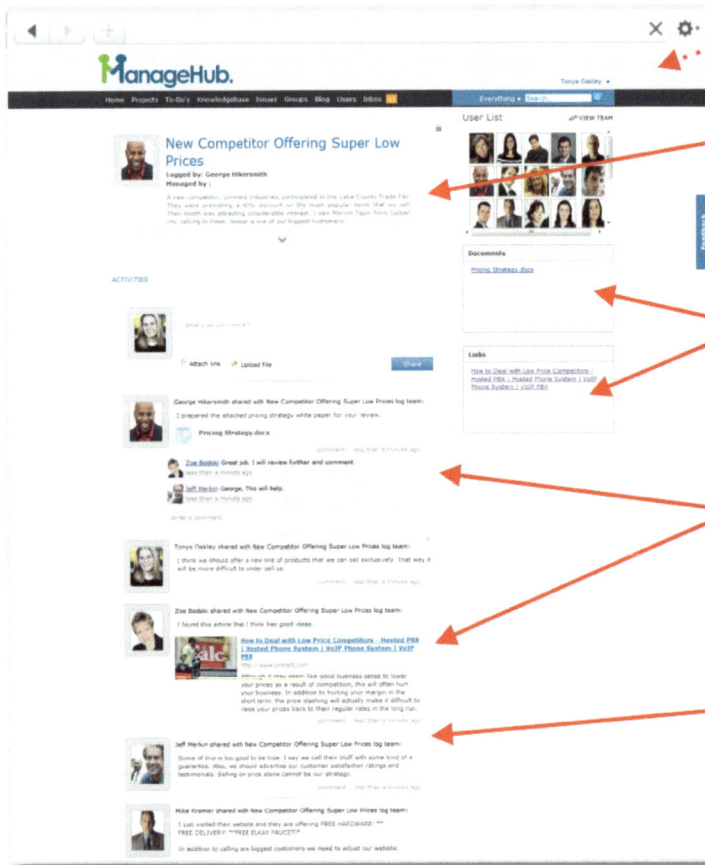

The discussion issue is clearly explained with details available in the pull down.

Link boxes provide you with handy access to attached documents, and external links.

The conversation flows with shared documents, link, and ideas.

Much better than the typical email exchange because everyone can see the conversation in one meeting room.

Use ComLogs instead of email and meetings: Every Communication Log has its own dedicated collaboration workspace that contains all related user comments and attachments. This enables participants to review the entire conversation thread at their convenience, whenever needed. It also allows new participants to join an active conversation without the need for a distracting "catch-up" phone call or meeting. Participants simply access the workspace and review the past comments, links, and attachments. Another advantage to using ComLogs is that the conversation is maintained as part of your company's historical archive. Resolved ComLogs can be searched and reviewed by subsequent teams when needed.

Collaboration must be facilitated: Department and process-team managers should frequently review all Communication Logs associated with their ManageHub workspaces to ensure members are actively discussing and resolving reported issues. When necessary, managers must prompt employees to participate, and hold process teams accountable for resolving the ComLogs.

Credit employees for reporting and resolving issues: Managers must regularly recognize both the employees who report valuable issues, and the process teams who resolve them. Public and private praise helps encourage employees to model your company's non-negotiable ManageHub behaviors. It celebrates your new company culture of innovation and continuous improvement. It also highlights the critical role that all employees play in fueling your company's continuous improvement cycle.

Reminder: Associate the ComLog with its department, process, and/or group: When creating a new Communication Log, (project or knowledge entry), be sure to associate it with its managing department, process, and/or collaboration-group. (See Note Below.)

Once the issue is saved, ManageHub will automatically alert related users with a system-generated email. The emails provide embedded links that invite recipients to contribute to the ManageHub discussion. If they prefer, recipients can simply reply to the email and their comment will be automatically posted back to the Communication Log workspace for all participants to see.

ManageHub will also alert users with clickable-listings on all related department, process, group, and user activity feeds. The cross-linked interconnection of project, knowledge, and ComLog workspaces with their related department, process, employee, and collaboration-group workspaces makes it very easy for you and your team to manage improvement throughout your organization.

Please Note: Use the same protocol to associate all Project and Knowledgebase entries with their managing department and process team. The drop-down link-lists are found on all popup setup screens.

When you create a new Communication Log be sure to associate it with its managing department, process-team and/or collaboration group.

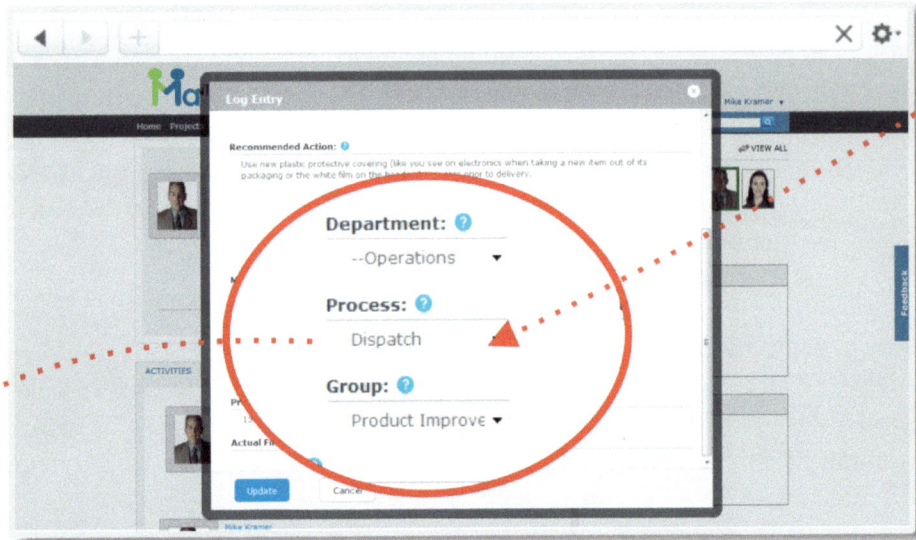

When saved, link-backs will appear in all related workspaces making it very easy for you and your team to find the information they need where they need it.

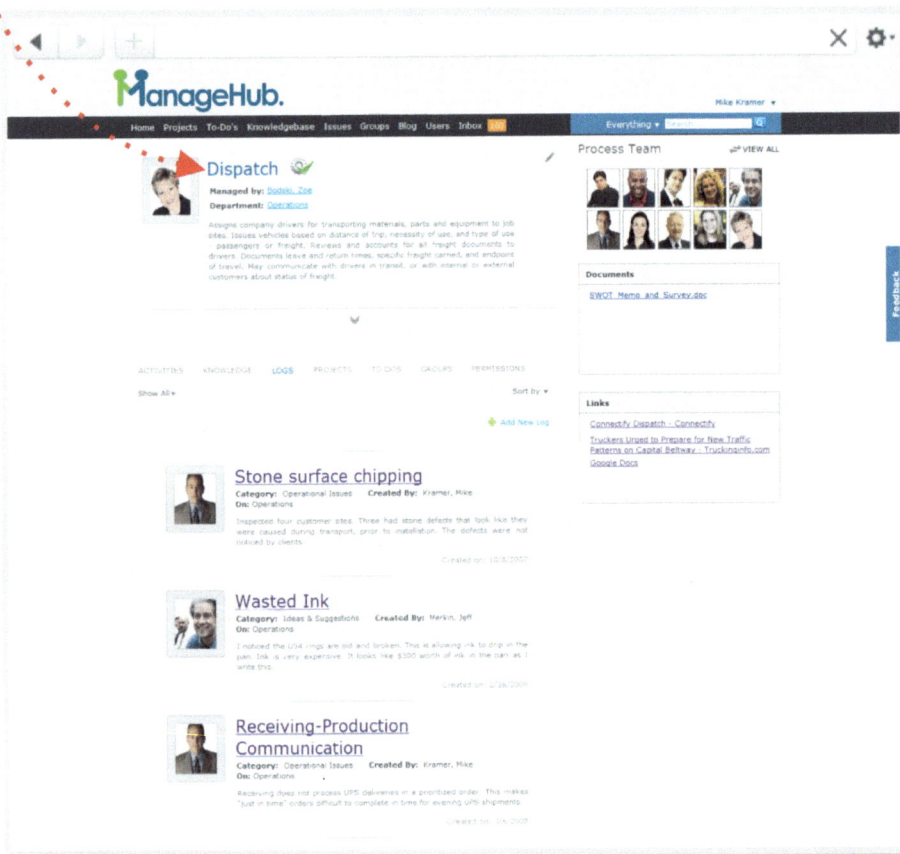

Use ManageHub to Create Your Company's Continuous Improvement Cycle

ManageHub automates your company's continuous improvement cycle. To illustrate how it works, consider the following scenario:

A front line employee is frustrated because she is wasting valuable time looking up warehouse location codes that could be easily added to pick lists generated by the company's sales order software. Correcting this issue would improve productivity, speed order processing and reduce cost. The employee used email to report her suggestion to multiple supervisors over the years. Promises were made but no action was taken.

Now consider the quick resolution that is possible when using ManageHub to automate continuous improvement. ManageHub facilitates communication between employees and process teams who are empowered to optimize and improve their procedures:

1. The employee reports her suggestion by creating a 💬 ManageHub Communication Log and associating it with the responsible department and process team.

2. The process team discusses the issue in the ComLog workspace. Several resources from the IT department are included in the collaboration. The decision is made to add the warehouse location code to the product database and add it to the pick lists generated during order taking.

3. The process team converts the ComLog into a 📋 ManageHub project to manage the steps necessary to implement the change.

4. The Order Taking process-team updates related procedures and training materials stored in the company's 📚 ManageHub Knowledgebase. The updates were automatically communicated to all affected employees in their ManageHub Newsfeed.

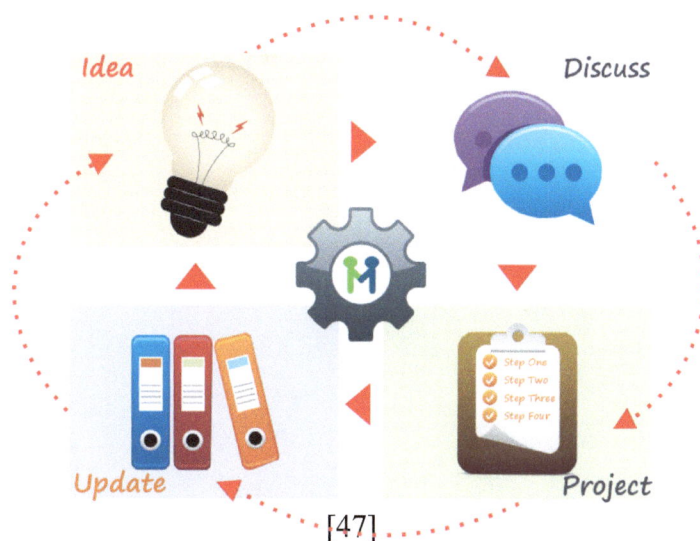

[47]

Using ManageHub, the issue was resolved quickly because front line employees from multiple departments were empowered to communicate, collaborate and resolve problems that related to their areas of responsibility.

The above scenario illustrates how (1) culture, (2) effective process management, and (3) open communication work together to optimize your company. It is simple and organic. It institutionalizes a culture of excellence. It leverages your employee's insights and creativity. It helps make your business flexible and resilient.

1 Idea

Your continuous Improvement cycle starts when one of your employees clicks on the icon to report an idea, problem, suggestion, or other important information.

2 Discuss

Every idea creates a discussion workspace where other users can help resolve the issue by sharing their insights, information, links and attach documents.

Link boxes provide you with handy access to attached documents, and external links.

The conversation flows with shared documents, link, and ideas.

Much better than the typical email exchange because everyone can see the conversation in one meeting room.

3

Project

With one click of their mouse, users can automatically convert a discussion workspace into a project.

Drag and drop task lists with cool click and slide animation.

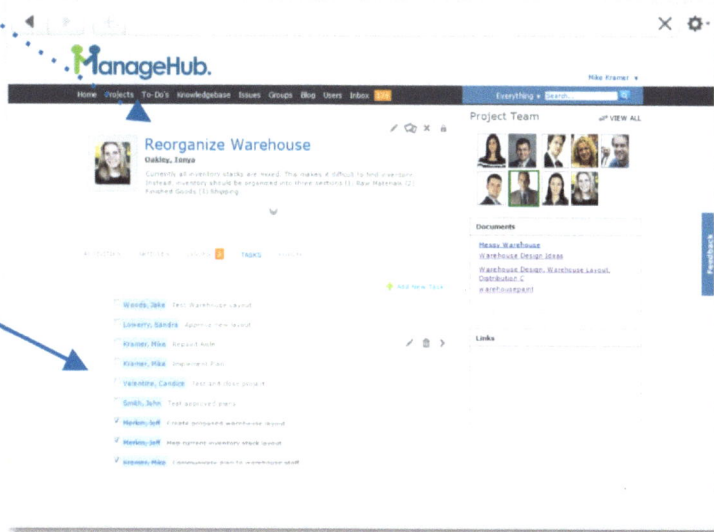

4

Update

Once the issue is resolved and the project (if necessary) is completed, the users can update all related knowledgebase entries. These may include: policies, procedures, training methods, strategic plans, and templates.

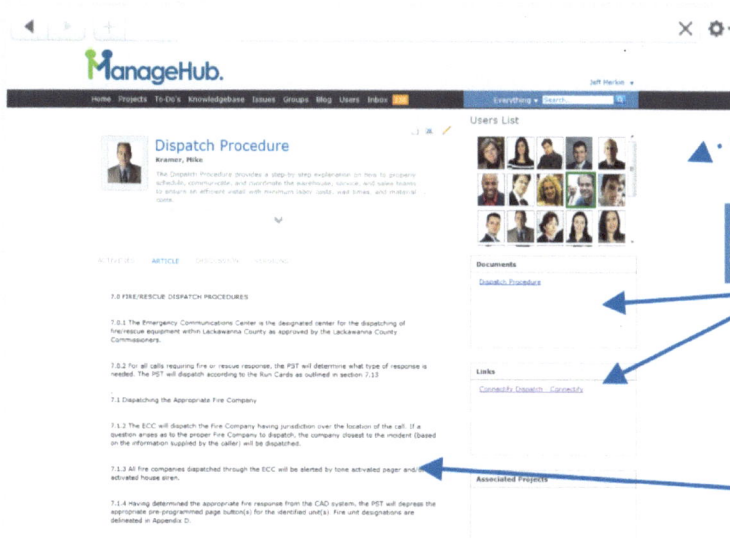

Link boxes provide you with handy access to attached documents, and external links.

Use the built-in text editor to update a policy, procedure, training plan, or other information.

You will likely need to dedicate 5-10% of your employees' time to improving your company. Consider it the cost of your freedom. The time your employees spend "fixing" broken processes should more than be offset by the time saved putting out the same fires over-and-over again. It is also a cost that should result in a significant return on investment. Your company will finally have a way to capture your employee's ideas for saving money, making money, minimizing waste, and increasing quality, consistency and customer satisfaction. Use ManageHub to document the projected and actual ROI (return on investment) of all communication logs.

As the leader of your company, it is your job is to manage the communication and collaboration. You are the catalyst, the change agent, and the conductor of all the moving parts. The next two chapters offer two techniques that you can use to engage your employees and encourage their active participation:

Chapter Five: Adopt a Culture of One-on-One Coaching and Mentorship
Chapter Six: Schedule Regular Accountability Meetings

Chapter Five:
Adopt a Policy of One-on-One Coaching and Mentorship

A company-wide program of coaching and mentorship is vital to creating a positive employee culture. When done correctly, it establishes two-way communication. It institutionalizes accountability and transparency. It increases performance of your company's non-negotiable employee behaviors, as listed in Chapter Two. It develops leadership skills. It also improves employee loyalty and retention.

Coaching sessions should occur frequently, at least once a week, during the startup phase of your ManageHub implementation. These initial sessions should focus on:

- Explaining why you are reinventing your company's culture.
- Answering questions, offering reassurance, and resolving resistance.
- Identifying employees who are enthusiastic early adopters.
- Providing ManageHub training.
- Encouraging employees to be active participants.

You can reduce the frequency of coaching sessions to once a month as your employees begin to consistently perform your company's non-negotiable behaviors, and meet your expectations. These monthly sessions should focus more on assessing your employee's progress, level of engagement, and setting learning objectives. However, you may need to increase the frequency of coaching sessions if you notice your employee slipping back into old behaviors.

Step-by-Step ManageHub Coaching Session Instructions

Use your employee's personal ManageHub workspace to structure a consistent coaching conversation. Your objective is to encourage them to become self-motivated, self-managed, high-performing, and high-value employees. Using their workspace demonstrates how they can use ManageHub to "coach" themselves.

Step 1 – Renew your relationship if it needs healing: Every work environment is complicated by an assortment of unique personalities. Even a usually harmonious working-relationship can become strained. Use your coaching/mentoring sessions to clear the air. If necessary, hire an experienced business coach to help mediate a problem, or help you and your employee mend fences.

Step 2 – Affirm your company's commitment to achieving excellent product/service quality and customer satisfaction: Set the tone for your coaching conversation by reinforcing your company's commitment to excellence. Discuss the benefits of maintaining clean and efficient operations. Remind your employees that your company's objective is to produce consistent high quality products and services that deliver an exceptional customer experience. For many organizations, excellence is already built into their DNA. Others will need to use coaching conversations, and team meetings to constantly reinforce this new and non-negotiable, cultural imperative.

Step 3 – Explain your motivation for implementing the ManageHub strategy: Change is hard for many employees to accept. Their first reaction is often to resist. Use your coaching sessions to win their support. Explain your good intentions. Share relevant principles with your employees. It is important that your employees understand that you want them to grow with your company as it grows.

Use your coaching sessions to explain that the fundamental logic of the ManageHub approach is to organize your company into self-managed process teams who are responsible for systematizing, standardizing, and continually improving the work they perform. Explain how this employee-centric approach creates a flat organization where every employee is a leader over their own work.

Explain the connection between continual learning, eliminating bottlenecks and job traps. Help your employees understand that documenting their own processes is the key to their being promoted. Explain that your ultimate objective is to create generations of leaders where you can hire new employees at the bottom and promote existing employees to the top. Finally, caution your employees that all the above benefits are just good intentions without their active participation.

Hopefully, your employees will sense your sincere desire to help them grow with your company. Hopefully, they will appreciate developing a trusting relationship with a boss that is guiding them to greater opportunity. Hopefully, they will return the favor with loyalty, dedication, and by optimizing their processes.

Step 4 – Communicate your company's set of expected behaviors: The success of your business optimization project depends on your employees *understanding and adopting* your set of non-negotiable ManageHub Behaviors. Discuss the rationale and benefits of each behavior. Explain how ManageHub tools and workspaces are designed to help them preform each behavior:

- Promote consistent product/service quality and customer satisfaction.
- Actively document process know-how.
- Share ideas and issues for improving the company.
- Participate in internal strategic projects.
- Actively learn new processes.
- Help coach, mentor and cross-train other employees in performing their processes.
- Actively participate on process and collaboration-teams.

Reviewing the list of non-negotiable behaviors helps set clear expectations for future performance. It also, sets the stage for the remainder of your coaching session. Refer to relevant behaviors as you review related sections of the employee's ManageHub workspace. Encourage your employee to use ManageHub to perform the behaviors.

Step 5 – Log onto your employee's ManageHub account: Ask your employee if they are comfortable using ManageHub tools and workspaces. If not, your coaching session is a perfect opportunity to provide one-on-one training and support.

Show your employee how to access their personal ManageHub workspace. Show them how to click on the home screen icons to create a knowledge entry, project, or

💬 ComLog. Show them how they can also click on the ➕ icon at the top of all tabbed workspace sections to create a new entry.

Use your coaching session to make sure your employee is familiar with their ManageHub home screen, tools, and workspaces. For example, help your employee create a 💬ComLog to report an idea or issue. Help them use the drag and drop link boxes to find their process team workspaces. Help them see how the ManageHub tools and workspaces bring your Breakthrough behaviors to life.

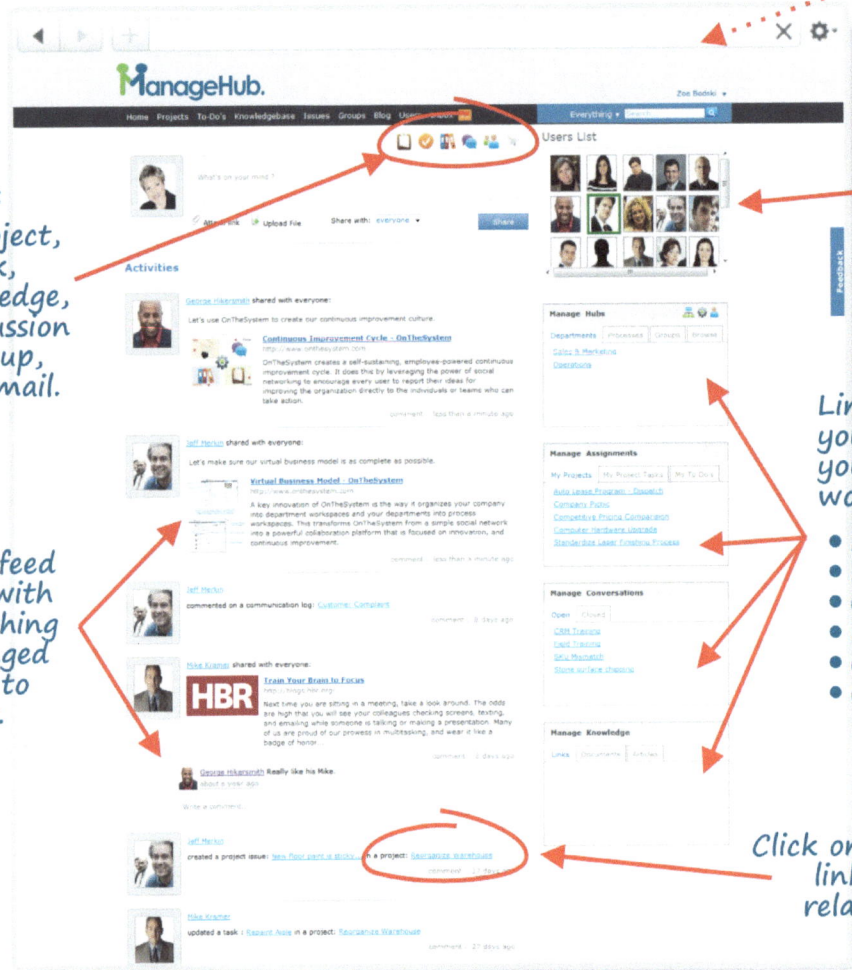

With one click:
- *Create a project,*
- *Assign a task,*
- *Share knowledge,*
- *Start a discussion*
- *Create a group,*
- *Send an in-mail.*

Facegrid connects you to everyone.

Your activity-feed provides you with links to everything that has changed that relates to your work.

Link boxes connect you to all of your collaboration workspaces:
- *Departments*
- *Processes*
- *Groups*
- *Projects*
- *ComLogs*
- *Groups*

Click on any activity-feed link to access the related workspace.

Step 6 – Review Your Employee's Workspace Header: Does your employee need help uploading their headshot photo? Have they added their contact information?

Update these setting by hovering your mouse over the employee's name on their home screen. Then click on the "Employee Setup" link located in the drop down list. From the Employee Setup screen you can:

- Update contact information.
- Setup email preferences.

- Integrate project and to-to tasks into your Google Calendar.
- Upload your headshot photo.

To update your user settings hover your mouse over your name and select the "Employee Setup" option from the drop-down list.

Use the Setup Screen to change your password, add your contact information, update your photo...

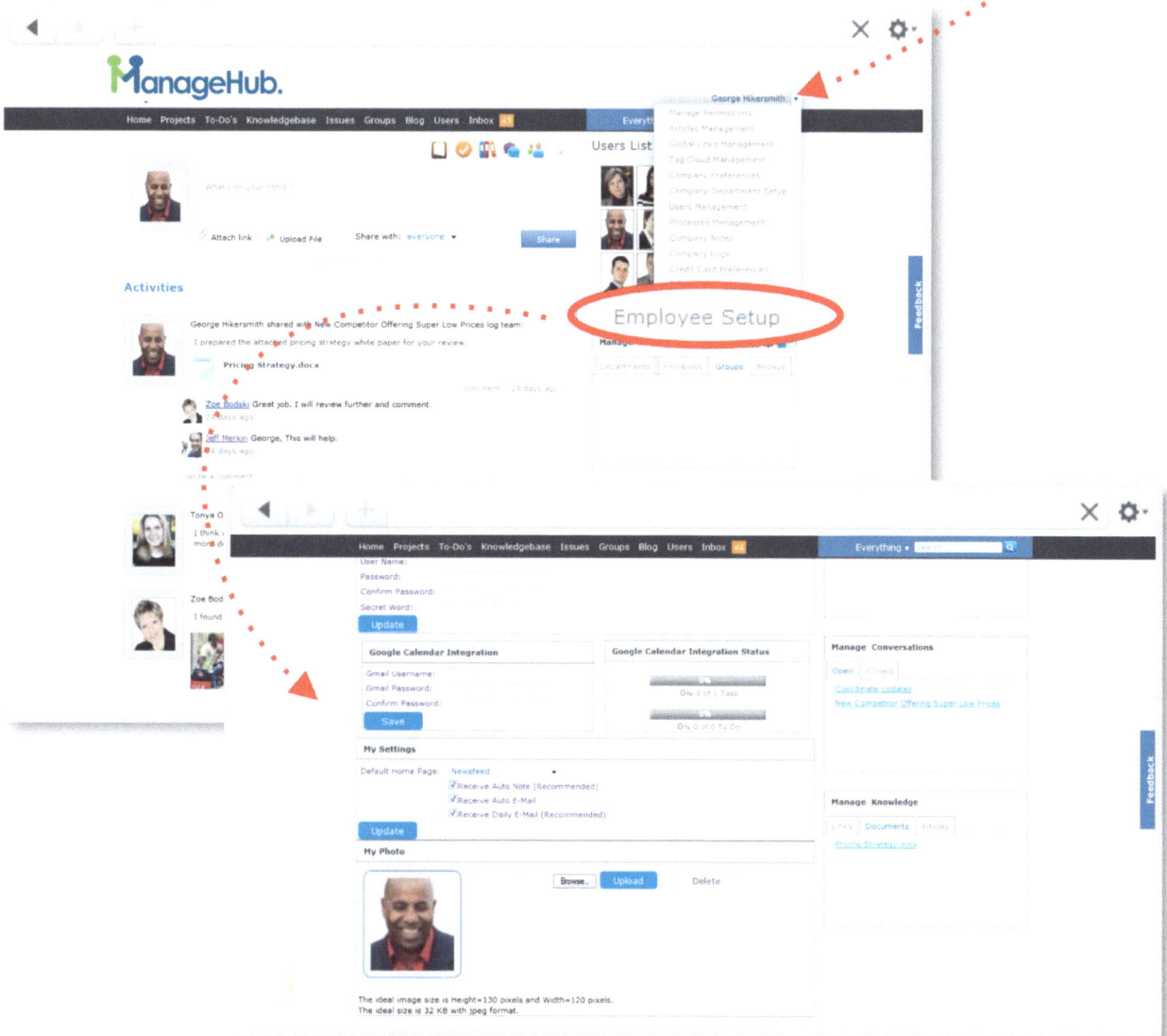

Step 7 – Review the Employee's Activity Feed: The content of your employee's activity feed is good first indication of their level of engagement. Scan the entries to determine if your employee created any new ComLogs, Projects, or Knowledgebase entries since your last coaching session. If so, be sure to review the items and praise your employee for their contributions. Also, be sure to scan the entries to determine if your employee is actively collaborating in existing Communication Log discussions. It is important to use the coaching sessions to encourage your employees to participate in any ComLog discussions that they can help resolve.

Review your employees Activity Feed to assess their level of engagement. Hopefully, you will find a variety of entries that indicate active collaboration including sharing ideas and contributing knowledge.

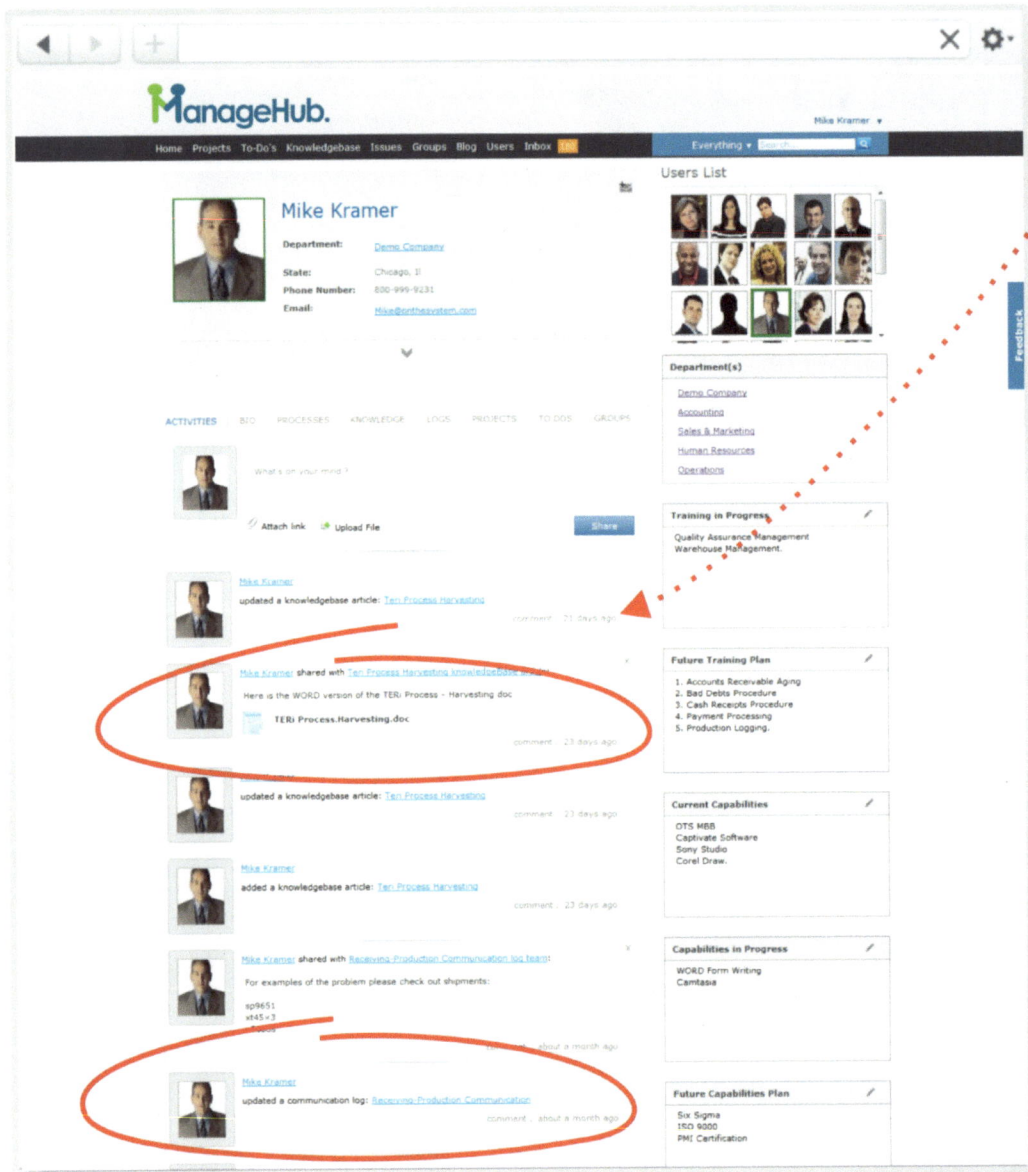

Step 8 – Review the Employee's Bio Tab: Is the employee's biography section completed? Does it provide enough information? The employee's Bio section should indicate an overview of their current responsibilities and past positions. Include descriptions of unique skills and experiences. Explain to your employee that the Bio section is searchable by managers who are looking for employees with specific abilities.

Show your employee how to click on the ✎ icon to add or modify information.

Step 9 – Review the Processes Tab: The Processes Tab lists your employee's processes. If they are a Process Manager, their photos will appear next to related links. The more processes the employee knows how to perform (and manages) the more valuable they are to your organization.

Ask your employee if the processes listed in their personal workspace are accurate and complete. If not, add the employee to additional process team(s) by reviewing the processes listed under the department workspace's process tab. If a process is not listed under the department's process tab, click on the ✚ icon to add the process.

Once you have determined that the employee's process list is complete, review each process workspace. Ask your employee if they are actively participating on the process team(s). Ask them if they are contributing knowledge and improvement suggestions. If not, use your coaching session to determine why they are not participating. Provide them with the training and support they need to become actively engaged.

If your employee is a Process Manager review the knowledgebase entries associated with the process workspace. Do they include all of the policies, step-by-step procedures, training methods, videos, schematics, flowcharts, and/or any other information that is needed to define the process's current standard of excellence? Are the listed knowledgebase entries sufficient to train a new process-team member with a minimum of direct support? Explain that it is your company's objective to minimize "job traps" that prevent promoting employees from within. If your employee is resisting sharing knowledge, remind them that if they are not *replaceable they are not promotable.* Be sure to acknowledge and praise employees who contributed valuable new knowledge.

Step 10 – Review the Knowledge Tab: The Knowledge Tab lists all the knowledgebase entries created by the employee. The more knowledge the employee shares the more valuable they are to your organization. Click on their knowledge links. Assess the quality of their contributions. If they have not contributed knowledge ask them if they have any knowledge to share. Click on the 📚 icon on their home screen, or the ✚ icon at the top of any "Knowledge" workspace section. Remind your employee to associate their knowledgebase entries with the appropriate department and process teams. This will ensure the knowledge links will appear on all related ManageHub workspaces.

Remind your employee that systematizing and standardizing the day-to-day processes of your business is a fundamental prerequisite to breaking through. It creates a sustainable company that is flexible and resilient. It establishes a benchmark (or standard) of excellence that can be continually improved.

Keep in mind that many employees will resist sharing their knowhow. They may horde their knowledge to increase their sense of "job security." Use your coaching sessions to help your employee think differently. Explain to them that, "If they are not replaceable they are not promotable." Explain to them that if they are the only employee that can perform a specific process they are likely to be stuck in a "job trap." Demonstrate your good intentions by creating a continual learning plan for the employee where they train to perform a new process while training others to perform their current processes. Your employee many need reassurance. They may have fears of being fired or losing influence. Let them know that it is your company's intention to multiply the opportunity of every employee that helps it grow.

Step 11 – Review the Logs Tab: The Logs Tab lists all the Communication Log entries created by your employee. ComLogs are used to share ideas and to report issues. The more ComLogs the employee creates the more valuable they are to your organization. Click on their ComLog links. Assess the value of their contributions.

If your employee has not created any ComLogs, find out why. They many have learned not to share their ideas. Perhaps in the past, their suggestions were dismissed, ignored, or not acted upon. In some cases their ideas may have been stolen by a manager, or they may not have been given proper credit. In other cases, the employee may never have been asked for their opinion, and he or she feels undervalued.

Use your coaching sessions to help your employee understand that it is your intention to create a culture of innovation and active employee participation. Explain how ManageHub relies on employee ideas to fuel your company's continuous improvement cycle. Encourage your employees to use ManageHub to share their ideas that can reduce waste, increase efficiency, or resolve recurring customer complaints. Ensure them that they will receive credit. Show them how ManageHub logs all their ideas and reports them on their personal employee workspace.

Ask your employees if they have any ideas or issues to share. If they do, click on the icon on their home screen, or the icon at the top of any "Log" workspace section. Remind your employee to associate their ComLog with the appropriate department and process teams. This will ensure the ComLog links will appear on all related ManageHub workspaces.

Step 12 – Review the Projects Tab: The Projects Tab lists all the Projects that the employee manages or performs one or more tasks. If they manage a project, their photo will appear alongside the related project link. The more Projects in which employees participate, the more valuable they are to your organization. Be sure to acknowledge and praise employees who participate in successful improvement projects.

Click on their Project links. Assess the quality of their contributions. Is the employee meeting their task due-dates? Are they helping resolve project issues? If the employee is a project manager, ask them to report their progress. Review the header section (including the pull down) and tabbed sections in the project's workspace. Are their projects healthy? Are their projects on budget? Are there any project issues that need resolution?

If your employee is not actively participating on project teams, remind them that there is a lot of work to be done -- *too much for a handful of employees to complete alone.* The most important project is your company-wide initiative is to systematize, standardize, and continually improve every operational process. Use your coaching conversations to encourage your employees to manage or participate on project teams. Explain that managing projects is an ideal opportunity to learn important management skills.

Step 13 – Review the To-Do Tab: To-Dos are one step assignments. They are a great way to keep track of the one-off tasks assigned to individual team members during meetings. Use them to hold employees accountable to their commitments. The To-Do Tab lists all the assignments that the employee is responsible for performing. The more To-Do assignments the employee manages the more valuable they are to your organization. Click on their To-Do links. Assess the quality, timeliness, and value of their work. Ask your employee to report on the progress of open items. Be sure to acknowledge and praise members who completed their To-Do assignments.

Step 14 – Review the Groups Tab: Groups are collaboration workspaces. They can be used to manage Special Interest Groups (SIGs), client engagements, cross department or cross organizational collaboration. Group workspaces can be populated with knowledgebase entries, ComLogs, projects, to-do's, and uploaded documents, and links. Group members are either invited or must be approved. It is sometimes helpful to review a Group's activity during a coaching conversation or team meetings. However, keep in mind that many Groups are private. This means that their activity is not known to all participants.

Step 15 – Create a Continuous Learning Plan: Use your coaching sessions to create a continuous learning plan for every employee. The learning plan should contain three elements:

1. Processes currently being performed (ManageHub automatically lists these in the "Processes" section of the employee's workspace).
2. Processes and capabilities employee are currently learning. (Click on the ✎ to edit the list in order of importance.)
3. Processes and Capabilities to be learned in the future (Click on the ✎ icon to edit the list in order of priority)

As you create and review an employee's learning plan, explain the connection between continual learning, creating a scalable organization, eliminating bottlenecks, and freeing them from their "job traps."

Keep in mind that some employees, especially old-time employees, will not be interested in learning new processes or skills. This is acceptable under two conditions: (1) You have enough employees cross-trained in other processes to avoid current or potential bottlenecks. (2) The employee is an active participant on their process teams where they help to systematize, standardize, and improve the process.

Every employee has a personal ManageHub workspace. The workspace organizes all of their work into tabbed sections. The more links that fill the sections, the more engaged the employee is in improving your company. Use the workspace to structure a meaningful coaching conversation.

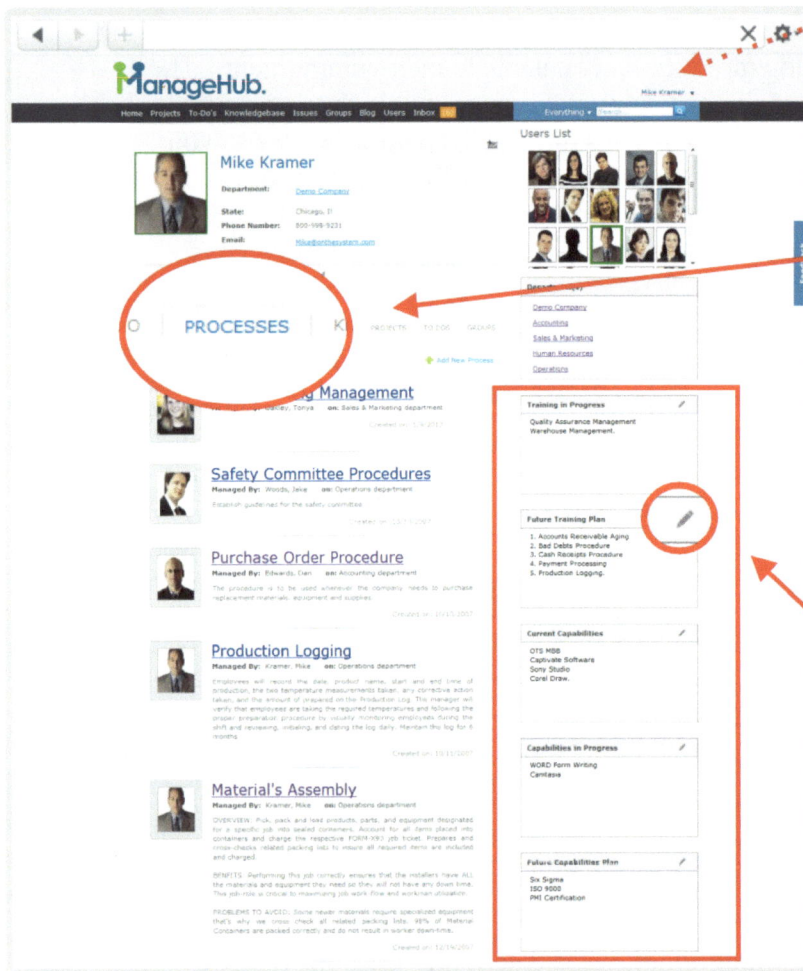

The "Processes" tab lists your employee's process-teams. The picture alongside each process link indicates the process-manager.

Use the editable windows to create a continuous learning plan for every employee.

Click on the icons to add content to each box.

Use your employee coaching sessions to assess progress and modify the plan.

As you help your employee create or modify their learning plan, remind them that it is not enough for an employee to learn new processes. They must also help train their fellow employees to perform their current processes. This helps create a dynamic learning culture that is not dependent on specific people performing specific work. It frees employees from potential job traps. It also creates a scaleable company that is prepared for rapid growth. Ask your employee if they are actively cross-training process-team members to perform their work.

Employee Coaching Worksheet

It may be helpful to use the following Employee Coaching Worksheet to track progress from session to session. The worksheet's sections mirror the tabbed sections in your employee's ManageHub workspace. Use the worksheet to take notes and highlight key points that you want to remember for your next meeting. Use the Values Alignment section to measure your employee's performance of your company's required ManageHub behaviors.

Employee Coaching Worksheet

| Employee Name | Jeff Zimmer |
| Mentor/Coach | Sally Smith |

ManageHub.
for the BreakthroughProject.com

Continual Learning Plan

Current Process	Processes in Training	Future Training
Reconcile bank statements	Input A/R Receipts	1. Payroll Processing
Approve/Input Vendor Invoices	Monthly Adjustments/Posting	2. Inventory update
Print Monthly Checks		3. Regulatory License Renewal
Prepare/Print/Send Customer Statements		4. Annual Audit "work-paper" preparation
Prepare Invoices		5. Weekly reporting
		6.
		7.

Switchboard Issues

We can improve collections if we age Accounts Receivables 15-30-45-60+ instead of 30-60-90-120+. By the time the account gets to 90 days it is unlikely we can collect. I think this can improve collections by $30,000 $60,000/yr.

We can save about 6 hours of work a month if we could integrate our accounting program with our bank.

Each line item on the sales order should be initialed, check-marked or circled to indicate that the item was delivered. When we send an invoice for back ordered items customers call. This makes them angry and wastes a lot of our time.

Projects

MGR?	Description
	Install, test and migrate data to new accounting program.
x	Reorganize regulatory filing system

Values Alignment

	J	F	M	A	M	J	J	A	S	O	N	D
Actively document your processes	x	x		x				x	x	x	x	x
Shares ideas and issues with Switchboard				x					x		x	x
Actively learning new processes								x	x	x	x	x
Helps cross-train peers	x			x	x	x			x	x	x	x
Promotes quality and customer satisfaction	x	x	x	x	x	x	x	x	x	x	x	x

A copy of the Employee Coaching Worksheet is downloadable from our information website at www.ManageHub.info/downloads.

Chapter Six:
Accountability Meetings

Schedule frequent general team meetings for all the employees who are participating in your ManageHub improvement initiative. The meetings serve three important purposes:

1. Build a positive culture.
2. Hold employees accountable.
3. Encourage use of ManageHub to perform non-negotiable employee behaviors.

Holding regularly scheduled team meetings is like the heartbeat for your company. They synchronize everybody to the same rhythm, and helps maintain constant, paced momentum. Meetings force everyone to pause and assess their progress.

The best meetings are short, focused structured and mandatory. The typical meeting length should be about 30 minutes or less. Keeping your meetings short is important to avoid push-back from your employees. The meetings should be structured using

MangeHub so that everyone knows what to expect. The meetings also need to be mandatory, (except for excused absences like vacations, unscheduled customer meetings, etc.), because you need everyone engaged, informed and involved.

To be effective, you should conduct your general meetings about once a week. Participants can meet in-person, online, or via conference calls. The meetings should use the following format:

Step 1 – Culture Building: Use your meetings to build a positive employee culture.

- Affirm your company's commitment to performance excellence.
- Make sure participants understand the logic and benefits of performing your expected employee behaviors.
- Explain that the logic of the ManageHub Approach is to organize your company into employee-managed process-teams.
- Encourage employees to share their knowledge using the ManageHub knowledgebase.
- Explain how using ComLogs to report their ideas and issues fuels your company's continuous improvement cycle.
- Communicate your expectation that everyone to be an active participant on their process-teams.

It many also be helpful in your initial meetings to conduct group ManageHub training.

Step 2 – Process Manger Reports: Strategically select a handful of Process Managers to report on their progress in documenting and improving their areas of responsibility. They should use their ManageHub Process Workspace to guide their presentation. (See Chapter Three for a step-by-step meeting plan.) Choose managers who have done a great job. Spend a moment to celebrate their success. Acknowledge their hard work. Make them a role model. You can also choose managers who are making significant headway systematizing and standardizing a particularly difficult process. Give them encouragement. Thank them.

Keep the meeting very positive and supportive. Never use the meeting to brainstorm solutions. Encourage use of ComLogs instead. If a process team is failing, do not use the meeting to offer support. This can pull your meeting in the wrong direction and fill the air with negative energy. Instead, provide one-on-one coaching between meetings.

Step 3 – Project Manager Reports: Strategically select a handful of Project Managers to report on their progress. They should use their ManageHub Project Workspace to guide their presentation. Discuss completed milestones (tasks) and report progress on resolving project issues. Choose projects that are strategically significant, and are on track to achieve their objectives. Spend a moment to celebrate their success.

Acknowledge the project-team's hard work. Make them a role model. Also, highlight important projects that are just launching. Give them encouragement. Thank them.

Step 4 – ComLog Reports: Next, select a few ManageHub ComLog workspaces to discuss. Choose ComLogs that can produce the most value. Thank the employee who reported the issue. Provide encouragement to the process-team who is responsible for resolving the issue. Let them know how much you appreciate their contributions.

Use the meeting to follow up on past issues that are still open. When helpful, encourage employees to collaborate on unresolved and inactive ComLogs.

Encourage your employees to create ComLogs to report their ideas for saving money, minimizing waste, improving efficiency, opening new markets, creating new products, increasing quality, and customer satisfaction. Explain how ComLogs fuel your company's continuous improvement cycle.

Step 5 – Other Company Business (Optional): Once the basic ManageHub portion of your meeting is completed you can discuss other company business. You can review financial results, report on sales opportunities, consider new strategic plans, etc.

The above, simple meeting format benefits your company in the following ways:

- Helps create employee-driven culture-change by focusing attention on engaged, empowered and active participants.

- Holds employees accountable to their commitments by requiring them to report their progress.

- Encourages communication, collaboration, innovation, and transparency.

- Credits employees with the ideas they communicate, the projects they manage and the knowledge they share.

- Promotes friendly peer competition. (Everyone wants to look good during the meetings.)

- Creates "generations of leaders" as employees learn how to manage teams and meetings.

- Speeds onboarding of new employees as they experience and adopt the meeting format.

- Ensures meetings are consistent and effective regardless of who leads them.

The meeting's format establishes your best practice culture. Benefits build over time as employees hear the same messaging repeated over and over again. They begin to internalize the importance of reporting their ideas and optimizing their processes.

CEO Scorecard Worksheet

Use the CEO Scorecard to plan your company's weekly Accountability Meetings. If you are a solo-entrepreneur, the scorecard doubles as a one-page strategic-plan. Use it to hold yourself accountable to your own business optimization objectives, and leadership responsibilities. You can also use it to structure meetings with your Business Coach, or to report progress to your peer mastermind group.

A CEO Scorecard template can be downloaded from our information website at: www.ManageHub.info/downloads.

The CEO Scorecard consists of the following sections:

Mission Statement: Your Company's mission statement describes the reason you created your business. For example, the mission statement of ManageHub.com is:

To dramatically improve the success rate of businesses by providing them with an easy onramp to adopting quality-management practices.

Writing a one sentence mission statement is best. It should be easy to remember and it should be inspiring. It should hint at your company's value proposition. It should also be used to guide your strategic planning process.

Vision Statement: Your Company's vision statement describes a utopic dream of what could be if you are able to achieve your mission. For example the vision statement of ManageHub.com is:

Create a worldwide business movement where innovation and growth results in prosperity for owners, employees, local communities, and national economies.

Again, one sentence vision statements are the best. They provide a long strategic view. They should be used to ensure that your strategic choices remain centered, focused and true to your beliefs.

Values Alignment/Leadership Scorecard: Your primary leadership responsibility is to establish and enforce use of your company's management framework. Your objective is to create the ultimate company culture of engaged employees who are committed to maximizing quality, customer satisfaction and performance excellence.

The following is a list of leadership behaviors that you must perform to meet your obligation. They are based upon the cultural guidelines and other concepts introduced in earlier chapters of this book:

- You actively promote a culture of quality, customer satisfaction and performance excellence.
- You enforce use of your ManageHub leadership framework.
- You actively coach/mentor your employees to embrace best practices.
- You and your employees meet weekly to report progress and hold each other accountable.
- You ensure that process teams are actively standardizing their work-activities.
- Employees are actively using the ComLogs to report their ideas for improving your company.
- Employees are actively managing and participating in improvement initiatives.
- You created Continual Learning Plans for every employee.
- Your business is becoming a meritocracy.
- You actively promote job sharing and cross training.
- You are actively eliminating current or potential bottlenecks.
- Your business is transforming into a flat, frontline, employee driven company.
- You are eliminating dependence on specific employees performing specific work.
- You are creating generations of leaders.
- When possible, you hire new employees at the bottom and promote existing employees to the top.
- Your business is sustainable, scalable and saleable.
- You engage outside resources when needed to coach, train, and support your employees.

Strategic Themes: Use the strategic themes section to list the broad company-wide objectives that you are trying to accomplish. Examples include:

- Operational excellence: Engage frontline employees to systematizing/standardizing every company processes.
- Product innovation
- Geographic expansion
- Customer retention/acquisition
- Employee engagement
- Quality culture

It is difficult to manage more than three strategic themes simultaneously. Strike the right balance. You do not want to overwhelm or underwhelm your employees.

Be sure that your department and process objectives are aligned with one or more of your strategic themes.

Chapter Seven:
The ManageHub Deployment Model

As much as you want to transform your business, you may worry that it is too late to fix your businesses. You *are* overwhelmed. You do not have any time to spare. Key employees are a source of endless problems. Retrofitting your company with the infrastructure it needs will add unwelcome complexity to an already chaotic situation. However, what are your options? Should you do nothing?

Many established companies avoid adopting quality management practices until it is too late. Some are replaced by newer, more sophisticated competitors. Some close their doors when an owner suddenly becomes ill. These businesses fail for the *wrong* reasons.

Other business owners have moments of clarity and determination. They launch their business optimization project but fail to follow through. They buckle under employee pressure. They become distracted by yet another business crisis. They may hire the wrong consultant or coach who takes them in the wrong direction.

It is better not to start a business transformation project than to start and not finish. Abandoning your business transformation project sends the wrong message to your employees. It tells resisters that they are still firmly in control. They are happy when you fail. It makes them bolder and meaner. You can see it in their "I told you so" smirks. It tells rank-and-file employees that you lack the determination you need to lead your business to real success. They wonder if your business can break through. Everyone becomes disillusioned, *including you.*

Abandoning your company's improvement project also makes future attempts at optimizing your business more difficult. Employees lose confidence that any business improvement approach can help. They roll their eyes at the mention of hiring another business consultant or adopting the latest business improvement craze. They see it as a big waste of time.

Use ManageHub to Engineer a Stealthy Business Transformation Project

Instead of promoting a grand initiative with lofty goals, consider engineering a quiet, grassroots revolution that flies under the radar of naysayers and troublemakers. Keep your lofty objectives to yourself. Gradually build momentum and support with tangible results instead of some distant, future promise of transformation. Make your "revolution" so simple and rooted in common sense that it barely needs an explanation.

Follow the steps outlined in this book. Start by reinventing your company's culture to appeal to your frontline employees. They have the most to gain from your business transformation initiative. They represent your future power base. They are looking for a way up. They are more likely to perceive working in your company as an opportunity. They offer you strength in numbers.

Next, systematically systematize and standardize your company's day-to-day processes. Optimizing your company's processes is the key prerequisite to building a sustainable and scalable business. Do this by organizing your frontline employees into ManageHub process teams. Your employees already perform their roles independently or in small groups, so formalizing existing relationships into teams should feel very natural. Create one team for every work activity in your company. Most employees will participate on multiple teams. Make the teams responsible for documenting and improving their areas of responsibility. Give them the authority and support they need to systematize and standardize every aspect of your company's day-to-day operations.

At the same time, use ManageHub to automate a simple continuous improvement cycle. Encourage every employee to use ComLogs to report their ideas directly to the process teams who can take immediate steps to improve quality, consistency, efficiency and minimize waste. You want to eliminate filtering by middle managers who may not understand the value of the information. Your goal is to have a continuous stream of employee suggestions power a continuous cycle of improvement and optimization.

Bring your business improvement process to life by initiating an ongoing conversation with your employees through individual one-on-one coaching and group accountability meetings.

This simple approach creates stealthy business-transformation. It gives you the freedom you need to adjust the speed of your deployment while staying fully committed to achieving your objective of performance excellence. It leverages the untapped skills, abilities, talents and insights of your most valuable and underutilized resource: Your frontline employees. It makes improving your business an ongoing, organic, natural process rather than something that is forced. It allows you to build unstoppable momentum that is only possible if you have a fully functioning management framework.

The ManageHub Quality Model: Incremental Deployment with the Potential for Exponential Impact

The ManageHub Quality Model offers your company a stealthy, socially-powered deployment approach. It can be used to improve any size or type of organization. It can also be used to optimize a department within a larger organization.

The ManageHub Quality Model starts by defining your company's capability requirements. These requirements mirror the non-negotiable set of ManageHub behaviors outlined in Chapter Two. Next, the quality model requires you to identify a step-by-step implementation plan beginning with a proof of concept test. The test is accomplished by applying the capability requirements to one or more process-teams. Your organization advances levels by successfully applying the capability requirements to the indicated percentage of processes managed by the related department(s).

To implement the ManageHub Quality Model, you must organize your departments into process teams, as explained in Chapter Three of this book. One member of every process team must be designated to be the process manager. The process manager is responsible for facilitating collaboration among process team members. Department managers oversee process teams and provide internal or external support, as needed. In most organizations, employees serve in multiple departments, and on multiple process teams as both members and/or managers.

ManageHub Quality Model

Department	Process Focus	Capability Requirement	Result

5 — 80%+ Optimized
- > All Departments
- > All Processes

> Apply a Holistic Leadership Framework to Each Department/Process Area

> Process:
> Operational processes are documented by policies, procedures, and training methods.
> Improvement objective(s) are established for every process.
> Action plans (projects/assignment) are implemented to achieve improvement objectives.
> Process teams collaborate to resolve process related issues.
> Quality audits (customer surveys, self assessments, etc.) confirm that process teams are performing according to company standards.
> Process teams manage a program of continual improvement for the work they perform.

Consistent Quality, Satisfied Customers, Engaged Employees, Preferred Vendor

4 — Remaining Departments
4=20%
3=40%
2=60%
1=80%
- > Key Process Area A
- > Key Process Area B
- > Key Process Area C
- > Key Process Area Z

3 — Department 3
3=20%
2=40%
1=60%
- > Key Process Area A
- > Key Process Area B
- > Key Process Area C
- > Key Process Area Z

2 — Department 2
2=20%
1=40%
- > Key Process Area A
- > Key Process Area B
- > Key Process Area C
- > Key Process Area Z

> Employee:
> Employees actively participate in documenting and improving the processes they perform.
> Employees actively report and help resolve process issues.
> Employees have a training plan that documents their ability to perform processes independently or with supervision.

1 — Department 1
1=20%
- > Key Process Area A
- > Key Process Area B
- > Key Process Area C
- > Key Process Area Z

> Leadership
> Leaders enforce use of the company's leadership framework.
> Leaders promote a "best practices culture" centered on quality, customer satisfaction and performance excellence.
> Leaders encourage employees to report and resolve issues.
> Leaders promote inter-company communication and collaboration.

0 — Proof of Concept Test
- > Apply the ManageHub Quality Model to one-five process areas.

Inconsistent Quality, Customer Issues, Employee Problems

Step 1 -- Define Your Organization's Capability Requirements: *Customize the Capability Requirements section for your organization.*

The Capabilities Requirements section of the ManageHub Quality Model reflect the essential elements of the most popular and respected management frameworks including Baldrige, ISO, TQM, CMMI, and EFQM. They also reflect the core behaviors outlined in Chapter Two of this book.

The Requirements are organized into three perspectives (Process, Employee and Leader). These three perspectives communicate a set of interrelated behaviors that are expected from all stakeholders:

Process:

- Operational processes are documented by policies, procedures, and training methods.
- Improvement objective(s) are established for every process.
- Action plans (projects/assignment) are implemented to achieve improvement objectives.
- Process teams collaborate to resolve process related issues.
- Quality audits (customer surveys, self-assessments, etc.) confirm that process teams are performing according to company standards.
- Process teams manage a program of continual improvement for the work they perform.

Employee:

- Employees actively participate in documenting and improving the processes they perform.
- Employees actively report and help resolve process issues.
- Employees have a training plan that documents their ability to perform processes independently or with supervision.

Leadership:

- Leaders enforce use of the company's leadership framework.
- Leaders promote a "best practices culture" centered on quality, customer satisfaction and performance excellence.
- Leaders encourage employees to report and resolve issues.
- Leaders promote inter-company communication and collaboration.

The Capability Requirements can be managed using the ManageHub software platform.

Step 2 -- Organize your people into process teams: *Setup your organization's departments, processes, and people on the ManageHub software platform.*

Day-to-day processes are the building blocks of your organization. If your organization's processes are efficient and continually improving, then your organization will likely be high performing. The problem in most organizations is that their employees are not formally empowered to document and continually improve the work that they perform. Typical problems include:

- Process know-how is siloed (and guarded) by process owners who do not share their expertise.

- Participants are not able to report and resolve issues that impact quality, consistency, and customer satisfaction. As a result, the organization spends valuable resources "putting out the same fires."

The ManageHub Quality model is designed to institutionalize a tradition of process documentation and continuous improvement. Processes are organized into teams. Each team works together to ensure that their process is:

- **Systematized:** Automated using software, checklists, machinery, log sheets, or some other method that ensures consistent quality of all output.

- **Standardized:** Employ written and/or video procedures and training-instructions to facilitate onboarding of new process team members with a minimum of direct instruction. The documentation should ensure uninterrupted operation of the process even in the event of key-member turnover.

- **Cross Trained:** Multiple employees are capable of performing the process. This reduces dependency on specific people performing specific work. This helps ensure the process is sustainable and scalable. It also frees team members for promotion as the organization grows and evolves.

- **Free of Bottlenecks:** Ensure the process is able to meet current, projected, and even unexpected or short-term increases in demand.

- **Optimized/Continuously Improved:** Process teams report and resolve issues that cause inefficiency, waste, customer complaints, etc.

A word of caution: Leaders often have difficulty defining their process teams. See Chapter Three for an explanation.

The ManageHub Quality Model flips traditional deployment plans that usually apply one capability requirement to the entire organization. This approach makes deployment difficult to manage and ROI difficult to measure.

Instead, ManageHub applies a holistic set of Capability Requirements to one process-team at a time. This allows your company to concentrate training and support to help ensure your people and teams really learn how to be your company's partners-in- quality.

Capability Requirement

> **Apply a Holistic Leadership Framework to Each Department/Process Area**

> **Process:**
> > Operational processes are documented by policies, procedures, and training methods.
> > Improvement objective(s) are established for every process.
> > Action plans (projects/assignment) are implemented to achieve improvement objectives.
> > Process teams collaborate to resolve process related issues.
> > Quality audits (customer surveys, self assessments, etc.) confirm that process teams are performing according to company standards.
> > Process teams manage a program of continual improvement for the work they perform.

> **Employee:**
> > Employees actively participate in documenting and improving the processes they perform.
> > Employees actively report and help resolve process issues.
> > Employees have a training plan that documents their ability to perform processes independently or with supervision.

> **Leadership**
> > Leaders enforce use of the company's leadership framework.
> > Leaders promote a "best practices culture" centered on quality, customer satisfaction and performance excellence.
> > Leaders encourage employees to report and resolve issues.
> > Leaders promote inter-company communication and collaboration.

Step 3: Proof of Concept Test: *Begin your ManageHub implementation with a low-pressure test.*

The success of any business-improvement initiative rests on the shoulders of its leaders. They must embrace the idea of creating a best-practice culture. They must clearly communicate their commitment to their team(s). They must establish clear expectations. They must stand firm against employee resistance.

Level Zero of the ManageHub Quality Model provides leaders with an opportunity to adjust to their new role as Capability Requirements champion-and-chief. They will need to be a teacher, evangelist, promoter, and enforcer.

Level Zero also offers your organization an opportunity to experience its learning-curve with a minimum of scrutiny and pressure.

Perform the test by choosing one to five process teams. It is preferable to choose teams from your Level 1 department but it is not required. It is more important to choose teams that are most aligned with the behaviors outlined in the Capability Requirements. One of your objectives is to create a core group of frontline employees who can help you mentor and support the onboarding of additional process teams. You also want to choose processes that require improvement, so that your organization can experience a measurable ROI.

Once you have assembled your teams:

- Meet to discuss the Capability Requirements. Make sure every participant understands the purpose of each requirement. Also, make sure they understand the interconnected behaviors, dependencies, and relationships between the Process, Employee, and Leader requirements.

- Encourage every participant to report any problems and ideas they have for improving their process including increasing quality, consistency, customer satisfaction, and eliminating waste. These issues should be reported using ManageHub Communication Logs. (If possible log onto ManageHub and create ComLogs together.)

- Encourage every participant to help resolve identified issues by logging onto ManageHub ComLogs and collaborating with their process teams. If needed, create one or more projects or to-do/assignments to resolve the issues.

- Instruct team members to identify an improvement objective for their process team. (Log onto ManageHub and update the process improvement objective together.)

- Task each team to systematize (automate) and standardize their process. They should be instructed to upload procedures, training methods, schematics, templates, and any other process-related documents to the processes team's ManageHub knowledgebase. If needed, offer the process teams the assistance of internal or external resources such as a trusted business advisor, Six Sigma specialist, automation expert, ISO, or process consultant. The consultants should guide and support the teams but not do their work.

[75]

- Instruct the process team to assign members tasks by using the ManageHub project management system and to-do assignment system.

- Remind all participants that implementing the ManageHub Quality Model is a team effort. The burden of implementation should be fairy distributed among all process-team members. The role of the process manager is to encourage member participation and to report progress. It is not to do all the work.

Business improvement does not happen in a vacuum. It requires changing attitudes and creating a culture of collaborating and innovation. Some team members will require significant encouragement and mentoring. The leader's responsibility is to support the process managers. When needed, step in and facilitate the process team's collaboration. Team members who are not active participants need to be mentored, coached, and if necessary, removed.

The ManageHub Quality Model suggests an incremental deployment approach that has the potential of exponential impact. Momentum builds as you move up the pyramid because you have more and more experienced employees who can mentor, coach, and support newly commissioned process teams.

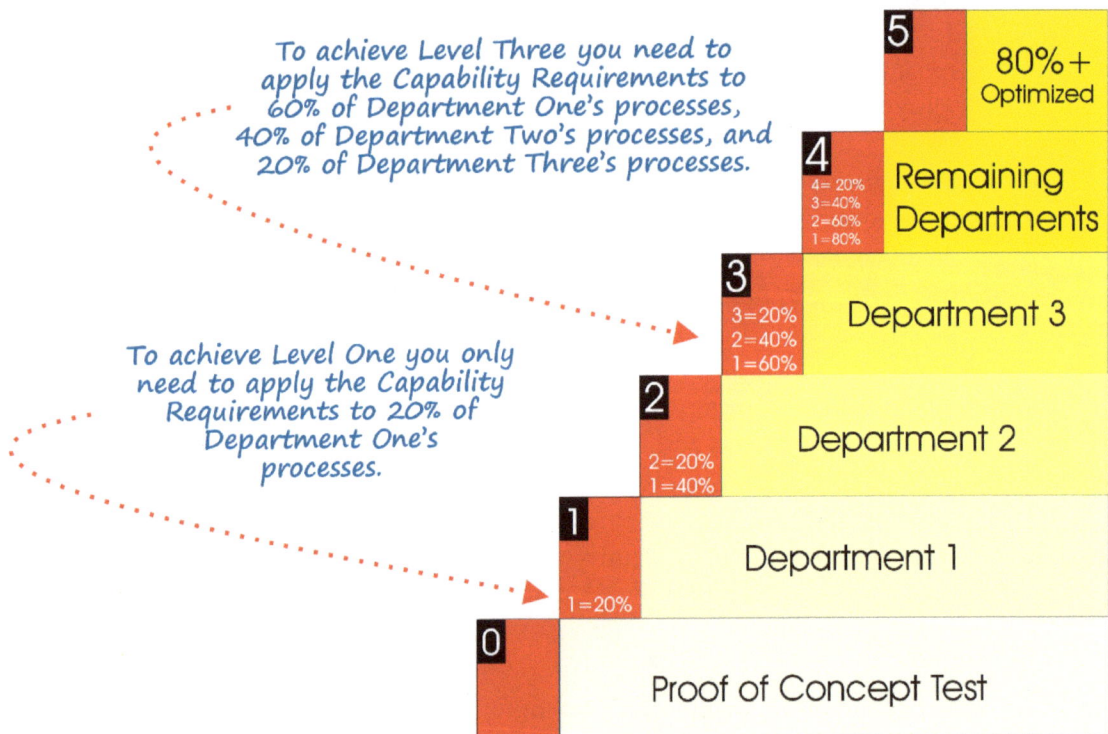

To achieve Level Three you need to apply the Capability Requirements to 60% of Department One's processes, 40% of Department Two's processes, and 20% of Department Three's processes.

To achieve Level One you only need to apply the Capability Requirements to 20% of Department One's processes.

5	80%+ Optimized
4	4= 20% 3=40% 2=60% 1=80% Remaining Departments
3	3=20% 2=40% 1=60% Department 3
2	2=20% 1=40% Department 2
1	1=20% Department 1
0	Proof of Concept Test

Step 4: Implement Levels 1-5: *Continue your ManageHub implementation by engaging additional process teams. Ask experienced members of optimized process teams to mentor and support newly formed teams.*

There is no set time limit associated with any of the ManageHub Quality Model levels. This provides your organization with the flexibility it needs to organize employees into process teams, familiarize the teams with the Capability Requirements, and offer needed training and support. Your intentions should be to move through the model with a minimum of stress, *and delay*.

It may take time to build momentum. This is especially true while implementing the first few levels of the model. Slower progress is also common in large or highly dysfunctional organizations. However, as you successfully engage more and more process teams you will be able to rely on a growing number of internal champions to help mentor and support the onboarding of new participants/teams. As a result, your organization's deployment momentum should build exponentially.

The ManageHub Quality Model offers significant advantages over traditional deployment plans that attempt to implement non-holistic change:

- Shortens the organization's learning curve and minimizes risks.
- Allows leaders to set reasonable expectations.
- Encourages employee participation.
- Allows internal and external resources to concentrate needed support.
- Helps the organization experience a measurable and replicable ROI.
- Offers the flexibility of adjusting the speed of deployment depending upon changing priorities or circumstances.
- Turns a growing number of employees into champions who can mentor and support additional process teams. As a result, succeeding levels move faster and faster, through the adoption.
- Institutionalizes a culture of collaboration, innovation, and continuous improvement.

A key to success is for you and all managers to actively use the ManageHub software. Log on to monitor progress, and contribute to Communication Log discussions. Encourage users to turn good ideas into projects. Also, start special interest groups and post blog articles that celebrate the success of your organization.

Remember, the purpose of your ManageHub software platform is to create your organization's management framework. It should be used to automate your management process. It creates your "company-way" of communicating, collaborating, sharing knowledge, resolving problems, managing projects, and eliminating waste. With consistent use, your ManageHub platform will become a virtual representation of your organization. You will be able to manage the big-picture, and drill down to manage the details

With proper use, you should see your organization's culture become more focused, innovative, and collaborative. Your people will become more engaged, self-managed, and self-motivated. Your processes will become better organized, and documented. Your organization will become more sustainable, scalable, and successful.

Rules of the Road

The earlier in your company's lifecycle that you adopt your company-wide management framework, the easier it will be to manage your business, innovate, achieve your objectives and grow. As you are about to take your first steps on your business improvement journey, use the following rules to guide you:

Keep it simple: Most quality improvement methodologies are overly complex and costly to implement. Many rely on statistical analysis and require extensive and expensive training. Your best approach is likely to apply the Pareto Principle, which is also known as the 80/20 rule. This rule states that you derive eighty percent of benefit from the first twenty percent of your effort.

Your first big benefit comes from creating a team of employees who share your commitment to building a GREAT company that is focused on achieving high quality, customer satisfaction and performance excellence. Your second big benefit comes from empowering frontline process teams to manage the systemization, standardization and continual improvement of their own areas of responsibility. Your third big benefit comes from creating a self-sustaining continual improvement cycle that is powered by ideas generated from your frontline employees.

Focus on ROI: Your business transformation initiative should result in a significant return on investment (ROI). An immediate return should come from optimizing and improving your day-to-day processes. Your Employee Survey and ComLogs should provide a rich source of ideas that save money, make money, eliminate waste and streamline your company's operational workflow. Every dollar you save adds a dollar to your company's bottom line. This means that even if you do not add any new revenues in the next 12 months you can still boost profitability by transforming your business into a lean-operating company. Ultimately, your greatest ROI will come from rapid growth that is made possible by having scalable infrastructure.

Make your ROI measurable by assigning a dollar value to every process improvement project, every strategic initiative and every ComLog suggestion.

Be a leader: You will likely encounter many obstacles. There will be moments when you want to give up and bend to the demands of powerful employees who resist you at every turn. You will likely experience unexpected crises that will push your improvement initiative to the back burner. Business is a battle. You need to stay steadfast, committed, determined and focused if you hope to win big. This is your moment of opportunity.

Avoid multiple approaches: A critical mistake that many business owners make is to simultaneously implement multiple business-improvement approaches. These owners are so enthusiastic about breaking through to their next level of success that they attempt every fad and engage every guru. This can result in conflicting messaging that overwhelms both you and your employees. A better approach is to choose one, holistic methodology that deploys tried-and-true best practices.

Stay stealthy: Make your business improvement process ongoing, organic and natural. Quality management practices should fit your business like a glove. They should feel right. You do not need to make big, bold announcements that can set you up for failure and embarrassment. It is often best to keep your big, transformational objectives to yourself and simply engage your employees in building a quiet revolution.

Enforce use of ManageHub: ManageHub automates your company's management function like accounting software automates your company's accounting function. It serves as your company's management framework. To be effective, your management framework must be used by *all* participants. This means that all of your stakeholders, from senior leaders to front line employees, must have access. It also means that all management activity must flow through your new ManageHub management system. If employees are allowed to sidestep using ManageHub, silos will reemerge and your desired outcomes will be lost. If, on the other hand, participants actively use ManageHub, your organization (no matter if it is large or small) can develop a powerful, "team language" that everyone uses to create strategies, manage projects, share information, document knowledge, assess progress, and improve communication and collaboration.

Seek the help of qualified professionals as needed: You are amazing, talented and passionate, but you do not know everything. You will likely need the support of experienced professionals who can help you and your employees systematize and standardize your business. You will also likely benefit from personal, one-on-one leadership and strategic coaching. You may not want to spend the money, but it is important to hold yourself accountable and to test the veracity of your decision making process. Consider it an investment in your future.

End Notes

Download the complete Management Toolset at:
www.ManageHub.info/downloads

Create your company's free ManageHub Account:
www.ManageHub.com

Join The Breakthrough Movement:
www.BreakthroughProject.com

---

[i] **W. Edwards Deming**, 1900-1993, Statistician, Author, Professor, introduced the Plan-Do-Check-Act Cycle

[ii] **Joseph Juran**, 1904-2008, The "father" of quality. Added a management dimension to statistical improvement.

[iii] *The Goal: A Process of Ongoing Improvement*, Eliyahu M. Goldratt, Jeff Cox, North River Press; 2nd Rev edition (1992)

[iv] *Good to Great*, James C. Collins, Harper Collins, Inc., New York (2001)

[v] *The E Myth*, Michael E. Gerber, Harper Business, (1988)

[vi] *Baldrige Performance Excellence Program*, NIST, 100 Bureau Drive, M/S 1020, Gaithersburg, MD 20899-1020

[vii] **EFQM**, 2 Avenue des Olympiades, 5th floor, 1140 Brussels, Belgium

[viii] **TQM**: http://asq.org/learn-about-quality/total-quality-management/overview/deming-points.html

[ix] **Kaizen** means "good change" in Japanese. It is a continuous improvement methodology popularized after WWII.

[x] **Six Sigma** is a statistical process improvement approach based on the work of Joseph Juran and popularized by Motorola and General Electric. A key tenant of Six Sigma is to remove variation from a process.

[xi] **ISO**, International Organization for Standardization ISO Central Secretariat 1, ch. de la Voie-Creuse CP 56 CH-1211 Geneva 20, Switzerland

[xii] **CMMI** Institute, 11 Stanwix Street, Suite 1150, Pittsburgh, PA 15222, U.S.